An artist's conception of the initiation of the Count and Countess Cagliostro into the secret rites presided over by the Comte de St. Germain.

THE MOST HOLY TRINOSOPHIA

OF THE COMTE DE ST.-GERMAIN

WITH INTRODUCTORY MATERIAL,
COMMENTARY, AND FOREWORD

BY

MANLY P. HALL

ILLUSTRATED WITH A COMPLETE PHOTOSTATIC
FACSIMILE FROM THE ORIGINAL MANUSCRIPT IN THE
BIBLIOTHEQUE DE TROYES

THE PHILOSOPHICAL RESEARCH SOCIETY, INC.
LOS ANGELES, CALIFORNIA 90027-2399

ISBN NO. 0-89314-417-7
L.C. 83-17214

Copyright © 1983
By the Philosophical Research Society, Inc.

Sixth Edition, Revised

Library of Congress Cataloging in Publication Data

Saint-Germain, comte de, d. 1784?
    The most holy trinosophia of the Comte de St.
Germain.

    Translation of: La très sainte trinosophie.
    Introductory matter in English; text in English and
French.
    "Illustrated with a complete photostatic facsimile
from the original manuscript in the Bibliotheque de
Troyes."
    1. Alchemy. 2. Cabala. 3. Manuscripts, French —
Facsimiles. I. Hall, Manly Palmer, 1901-1990

II. Title.
QD25.S153   1983   133   83-17214
ISBN 0-89314-417-7

Dustjacket design by Anne Shields.

Published by
THE PHILOSOPHICAL RESEARCH SOCIETY, INC.
3910 Los Feliz Boulevard, Los Angeles, CA 90027
Printed in the U.S.A.

TABLE OF CONTENTS

FOREWORD

————oOo————

PART ONE

THE MAN WHO DOES NOT DIE

————oOo————

PART TWO

THE RAREST OF OCCULT MANUSCRIPTS

————oOo————

PART THREE

COMPLETE PHOTOSTATIC FACSIMILE
OF THE ORIGINAL MANUSCRIPT OF THE
MOST HOLY TRINOSOPHIA

————oOo————

PART FOUR

NOTES AND COMMENTARIES

Curieux scrutateur de la Nature entière,
  J'ai connu du grand tout le principe et la fin.
J'ai vu l'or en puissance au fond de sa rivière
  J'ai saisi sa matière et surpris son levain.

J'expliquai par quel art l'âme aux flancs d'une mère
  Fait sa maison, l'emporte, et comment un pépin
Mis contre un grain de blé, sous l'humide poussière;
  L'un plante et l'autre cep, sont le pain et le vin.

Rien n'était, Dieu voulant, rien devint quelque chose,
  J'en doutais, je cherchai sur quoi l'univers pose.
  Rien gardait l'équilibre et servait de soutien.

Enfin avec le poids de l'éloge et du blâme
  Je pesai l'éternel; il appella mon âme:
  Je mourrai, j'adorai, je ne savais plus rien.

—Comte de St.-Germain

FOREWORD

An interesting reference to St. Germain appeared in the *London Chronicle*, May 31 to June 3, 1760, under the title "Anecdotes of a Mysterious Stranger," "From Germany he carried into France the reputation of a high and sovereign alchymist, who possessed the secret powder, and in consequence the universal medicine. The whisper ran the stranger could make gold. The expence at which he lived seemed to confirm that account; but the minister at that time, to whom the matter had been whispered as important, smiling answered he would put it on a short issue. He ordered an enquiry to be made whence the remittances he [St. Germain] received came, and told those who had applied to him that he would soon show them what quarries they were which yielded this philosopher's stone. The means that great man took to explain the mystery, though very judicious, served only to increase it; whether the stranger had accounts of the enquiry that was ordered and found means to evade it, and by what other accident 'tis not known, but the fact is that in the space of two years, while he was thus watched, he lived as usual, paid for everything in ready money, and yet no remittance came into the kingdom for him." (Reprinted on pages 95-96, *Secret Societies and the French Revolution* by Una Birch.)

Numerous authors can be quoted who had some passing acquaintance with the Comte de St. Germain. Most of the incidents recorded, however, give no insight into his religious or philosophical convictions, or the secret instructions which he is said to have given to a small circle of accepted disciples.

Both *La Très Sainte Trinosophie* in the Bibliotheque de Troyes in France and the cipher manuscript *La Magie*

FOREWORD

Sainte in the Library of our Society are devoted entirely to the deeper secrets of the esoteric tradition. It is reported that a third manuscript also exists and, according to Lionel Hauser, member of the Ancien Membre du Conseil de Direction de La Société Théosophique de France, is in the collection of a highly illuminated man residing in the south of France.

Les Mystères de la Science by Louis Figuier, Paris: 1881?, includes an artist's conception of the initiation of the Count and Countess Cagliostro into the secret rites presided over by the Comte de St. Germain. This picture seems to have been inspired by a description which appeared in *Memoires Authentique pour Servir a l'Histoirie du Comte de Cagliostro.* This book was published anonymously in 1785, but is generally attributed to the Marquis de Luchet. According to this little volume, Cagliostro had requested the favor of a secret audience with St. Germain for himself and his wife.

The meeting was set for 2:00 A.M. The sanctuary was lighted with hundreds of candles and St. Germain sat on an altar in the midst of the room. In the course of the ritual, a mysterious book was opened and Cagliostro listened while his own future was read to him with a detailed description of his persecution, trial, dishonor, and imprisonment. In *A Modern Panarion*, H.P. Blavatsky writes of St. Germain, "The treatment this great man, this pupil of Indian and Egyptian hierophants, this proficient in the secret wisdom of the East, has had from Western writers, is a stigma upon human nature."

In many European countries, especially France and Germany, there was a strong revival of esoteric beliefs in the second half of the eighteenth century. The political confusion of that time inspired many thoughtful persons to explore the wisdom of the ancient world. The miraculous convictions were supported by references to the Alexandrian school which interpreted the theology of the later Egyptians in terms of magic and metaphysics. There was a strong revival of Rosicrucianism, alchemy, astrology, the Hermetic arts, cabalism, and ceremonial magic. A considerable literature appeared and the gullibility of the credulous was exploited for private profit.

Although St. Germain functioned in the midst of the prevailing confusion of such doctrines, he was untouched by the popular psychism. He was never accused of fraud, though many efforts were made to damage his reputation. His abilities and accomplishments were the wonders of his time. Here was a celebrated person, moving in the highest circles of society who was a talented artist, a skilled musician, a proficient chemist, and a devout student of those yogic and tantric disciplines which he studied and mastered and which he is believed to have learned while traveling in India with Lord Clive. While in the company of scholars, he proved himself to be proficient in nearly every branch of learning.

St. Germain was credited with an extraordinary memory which he said was disciplined by regular reading from *Il Pastor Fido* by Battista Guarini (1538-1612), the celebrated Italian Renaissance court poet. After a more or less unfortunate association with the Duke of Ferrara, he retired to his ancestral farm and wrote *Il Pastor Fido (The Faithful Shepherd)*. Guarini was a controversialist and, like Tasso, favored a universal reformation of human society. The *Pastor Fido* has a strong rococo quality. It is elegant and was dramatized several times. It is said to have inspired

FOREWORD

The Faithful Shepherdess by John Fletcher.

The present work gives some indication of St. Germain's knowledge of obscure sciences. As may be expected, part of the manuscript is in cipher and there is no obvious key to the cryptic alphabet. There are Gnostic symbols and some illustrations that also seem to suggest the Greek Mysteries. The nineteenth century French schools of Eliphas Levi, De Guaita, and Papus seem to have inherited much of their symbolism from the eighteenth century revival of the ancient wisdom. Many students of the esoteric sciences seem to be unaware of those French schools which were strongly committed to secret arts and sciences.

Although nearly two hundred years have passed since his death or disappearance, research into the character and career of St. Germain continues. He was called "the man who does not die," and it is certain that interest in him is still very much alive. He belonged to a tradition which many persons want to believe. He bears witness to the possibility of immortality and the attainment of wisdom. St. Germain was an initiate of the Mystery Tradition and must be included among those whom the Rosicrucians called servants of the Generalissimo of the World and faithful secretaries of Nature.

MANLY P. HALL

THE MAN WHO DOES NOT DIE

 HE great Illuminist, Rosicrucian and Freemason who termed himself the Comte de St.-Germain is without question the most baffling personality of modern history. His name was so nearly a synonym of mystery that the enigma of his true identity was as insolvable to his contemporaries as it has been to later investigators. No one questioned the Comte's noble birth or illustrious estate. His whole personality bore the indelible stamp of gentle breeding. The grace and dignity that characterized his conduct, together with his perfect composure in every situation, attested the innate refinement and culture of one accustomed to high station.

A London publication makes the following brief analysis of his ancestry: "Did he in his old age tell the truth to his protector and enthusiastic admirer, Prince Charles of Hesse Cassel? According to the story told by his last friend, he was the son of Prince Rakoczy, of Transylvania, and his first wife, a Takely. He was placed, when an infant, under the protection of the last of the Medici (Gian Gastone). When he grew

IX

up and heard that his two brothers, sons of the Princess Hesse Rheinfels, of Rothenburg, had received the names of St. Charles and St. Elizabeth, he determined to take the name of their holy brother, St. Germanus. What was the truth? One thing alone is certain, that he was the protege of the last Medici." Caesare Cantu, librarian at Milan, also substantiates the Rakoczy hypothesis, adding that St.-Germain was educated in the University at Siena.

In her excellent monograph, *The Comte de St.-Germain, the Secret of Kings,* Mrs. Cooper-Oakley lists the more important names under which this amazing person masqueraded between the years 1710 and 1822. "During this time," she writes, "we have M. de St.-Germain as the Marquis de Montferrat, Comte Bellamarre or Aymar at Venice, Chevalier Schoening at Pisa, Chevalier Weldon at Milan and Leipzig, Comte Soltikoff at Genoa and Leghorn, Graf Tzarogy at Schwalback and Triesdorf, Prinz Ragotzky at Dresden, and Comte de St.-Germain at Paris, The Hague, London, and St. Petersburg." To this list it may be added that there has been a tendency among mystical writers to connect him with the mysterious Comte de Gabalais who appeared to the Abbe Villiers and delivered several discourses on sub-mundane spirits. Nor is it impossible that he is the same as the remarkable Signor Gualdi whose exploits Hargrave Jennings recounts in his book *The Rosicrucians, Their Rites and Mysteries.* He is also suspected of being identical with Count Hompesch the last Grand Master of the Knights of Malta.

In personal appearance, the Comte de St.-Germain has been described as of medium height, well proportioned in body and of regular and pleasing features. His complexion was somewhat swarthy and his hair dark, though often powdered. He dressed simply, usually in black, but his clothes were well fitting and of the best quality. His eyes possessed a great fascination and those who looked into them were profoundly influenced. According to Madame de Pompadour, he claimed to possess the secret of eternal youth, and upon a certain occasion claimed having been personally acquainted with Cleopatra, and at another time of having "chatted familiarly with the Queen of Sheba!" Had it not been for his striking personality and apparently supernatural powers, the Comte would undoubtedly have been considered insane, but his transcending genius was so evident that he was merely termed eccentric.

From *Souvenirs de Marie Antoinette,* by Madame la Comtesse d'Adhemar, we have an excellent description of the Comte, whom Frederick the Great referred to as "the man who does not die": "It was in 1743 the rumour spread that a foreigner, enormously rich, judging by the magnificence of his jewelry, had just arrived at Versailles. Where he came from, no one has ever been able to find out. His figure was well-knit and graceful, his hands delicate, his feet small, and the shapely legs enhanced by well-fitting silk stockings. His nether garments, which fitted very closely, suggested a rare perfection of form. His smile showed magnificent teeth, a pretty dimple marked his chin, his hair was black, and his glance soft and penetrating. And, oh, what eyes! Never have I seen their like. He looked about forty or forty-five years old. He was often to be met within the royal private apartments, where he had unrestricted admission at the beginning of 1768."

The Comte de St.-Germain was recognized as an outstanding scholar and linguist of his day. His linguistic proficiency verged on the supernatural. He spoke German, English, Italian, Portuguese, Spanish, French with a Piedmontese accent, Greek, Latin, Sanskrit, Arabic and Chinese with such fluency that in every land in which he visited he was accepted as a native. "Learned," writes one author, "speaking every civilized language admirably, a great musician, an excellent chemist, he played the part of a prodigy and played it to perfection." Even his most relentless detractors admitted that the Comte was possessed of almost incredible attainments in every department of learning.

Madame de Pompadour extols the genius of St.-Germain in the following words: "A thorough knowledge of all languages, ancient and modern; a prodigious memory; erudition, of which glimpses could be caught between the caprices of his conversation, which was always amusing and occasionally very engaging; an inexhaustible skill in varying the tone and subjects of his converse; in being always fresh and in infusing the unexpected into the most trivial discourses made him a superb talker. Sometimes he recounted anecdotes of the court of the Valois or of princes still more remote, with such precise accuracy in every detail as almost to create the illusion that he had been an eyewitness to what he narrated. He had traveled the whole world over and the king lent a willing ear to the narratives of his voyages over Asia and Africa, and to his tales about the courts of Russia, Turkey and Austria. He appeared to be more intimately acquainted with the secrets of each court than the *charge d'affaires* of the king."

The Comte was ambidextrous to such a degree that he could write the same article with both hands simultaneously. When the two pieces of paper were afterwards placed one upon the other with the light behind them the writing on one sheet exactly covered the writing on the other. He could repeat pages of print after one reading. To prove that the two lobes of his brain could work independently he wrote a love letter with his right hand and a set of mystical verses with his left, both at the same time. He also sang beautifully.

By something akin to telepathy this remarkable person was able to feel when his presence was needed in some distant city or state and it has even been recorded of him that he had the disconcerting habit of appearing in his own apartments and those of his friends without resorting to the conventionality of the door.

He was, by some curious circumstance, a patron of railroads and steamboats. Franz Graeffer, in his *Recollections of Vienna*, recounts the following incident in the life of the astonishing Comte: "St.-Germain then gradually passed into a solemn mood. For a few seconds he became rigid as a statue; his eyes, which were always expressive beyond words, became dull and colourless. Presently, however, his whole being became reanimated. He made a movement with his hand as if in signal of departure, then said 'I am leaving (ich scheide) do not visit me. Once again will you see me. Tomorrow night I am off; I am much needed in Constantinople, then in England, there to prepare two inventions which you will have in the next century—trains and steamboats.' "

As an historian the Comte possessed an uncanny knowledge of every occurrence of the preceding two thousand years and in his reminiscences he described in intimate detail events of the previous centuries in which he had played important roles. "He spoke of scenes at the court of Francis I as if he had seen them, describing exactly the appearance of the king, imitating his voice, manner and language—affecting throughout the character of an eyewitness. In like style he edified his audience with pleasant stories of Louis XIVth, and regaled them with vivid descriptions of places and persons." (*See All the Year Round*).

Most of St.-Germain's biographers have noted his peculiar habits with regard to eating. It was diet, he declared, combined with his marvellous elixir, which constituted the true secret of longevity, and although invited to the most sumptuous repasts he resolutely refused to eat any food but such as had been specially prepared for him and according to his recipes. His food consisted mostly of oatmeal, groats and the white meat of chicken. He is known on rare occasions to have taken a little wine and he always took the most elaborate precautions against the possibility of contracting cold. Frequently invited to dinner, he devoted the time during which he naturally should have eaten to regaling the other guests with tales of magic and sorcery, unbelievable adventures in remote places and intimate episodes from the lives of the great.

In one of his tales concerning vampires, St.-Germain mentioned in an offhand way that he possessed the wand or staff with which Moses brought water from the rock, adding that it had been presented to him at Babylon during the reign of Cyrus the Great. The memoir writers admit themselves at a loss as to how many of the Comte's statements could be believed. Common sense, as then defined, assured them that most of the accounts must be fashioned out of whole cloth. On the other hand, his information was of such precise nature and his learning so transcendent in every respect that his words carried the weight of conviction. Once while relating an anecdote regarding his own experiences at some remote time and suddenly failing to recollect clearly what he considered a relevant detail, he turned to his valet and said, "Am I not mistaken, Roger?" The good man instantly replied: "Monsieur le Comte forgets that I have only been with him for five hundred years. I could not, therefore, have been present at that occasion. It must have been my predecessor."

The smallest doings of so unusual a person as St.-Germain would, of course, be meticulously noted. Several interesting and amusing bits of information are available relative to the establishment which he maintained in Paris. He had two valets de chambre. The first, Roger, already mentioned, and the second a Parisian engaged for his knowledge of the city and other useful local information. "Besides this, his household consisted of four lackeys in snuff-colored livery and gold braiding. He hired a carriage at five hundred francs a month. As he often changed his coats and waistcoats, he had a rich and expensive collection of them but nothing approached the magnificence of his buttons, studs, watches, rings, chains, diamonds, and other precious stones. Of these he possessed a very large value and varied them every week."

Meeting St.-Germain one day at dinner Baron Gleichen chanced to focus the conversation upon Italy and had the good fortune to please St.-Germain, who, turning to him remarked: "I have taken a great fancy to you, and will show you a dozen pictures, the like of which you have not seen in Italy." In the words of Gleichen: "Actually, he almost kept his word, for the pictures he showed me were all stamped either with singularity or perfection, which rendered them more interesting than many first-class works. Above all was a Holy Family by Murillo, equal in beauty to that by Raffaello at Versailles. But he showed me other wonders—a large quantity of jewels and colored diamonds of extraordinary size and perfection. I thought I beheld the treasures of the Wonderful Lamp. Among other gems were an opal of monstrous size, and a white sapphire (?) as large as an egg, which, by its brilliancy, dimmed all the stones compared with it. I flatter myself that I am a connoisseur in gems, but I can declare that it was impossible to perceive any reason for doubting the genuineness of these jewels, the more so that they were not mounted."

As an art critic St.-Germain could instantly detect the most cleverly perpetrated forgeries. He did considerable painting himself, achieving an incredible brilliance of color. He was so successful that Vanloo the French artist begged him to divulge the secret of his pigments but he refused. He is accredited with having secured astonishing results in the painting of jewelry by mixing powdered mother-of-pearl with his colors. What occurred to his priceless collection of paintings and jewels after his death or disappearance is unknown. It is possible that the Comte's chemical knowledge comprehended the manufacture of luminous paint such as is now used on watch dials. His skill as a chemist was so profound that he could remove flaws from diamonds and emeralds, which feat he actually performed at the request of Louis XV in 1757. Stones of comparatively little value were thus transformed into gems of the first water after remaining for a short time in his possession. He frequently performed this last experiment, if the statements of his friends can be relied upon. There is also a popular story to the effect that he placed gems worth thousands of dollars on the place cards at the banquets he gave.

It was in the court at Versailles that the Comte de St.-Germain was brought face to face with the elderly Comtesse de Gergy. Upon beholding the celebrated magician, the aged lady stepped back in amazement and the following well-authenticated conversation took place between the two:

"Fifty years ago," the Comtesse said, "I was ambassadress at Venice and I remember seeing you there looking just as you do now, only somewhat riper in age perhaps, for you have grown younger since then."

Bowing low, the Comte answered with dignity: "I have always thought myself happy in being able to make myself agreeable to the ladies."

Madame de Gergy then continued: "You then called yourself the Marquis Balletti."

The Comte bowed again and replied: "And Comtesse
Gergy's memory is still as good as it was fifty years ago."

The Comtesse smiled. "That I owe to an elixir you gave
me at our first meeting. You are really an extraordinary man."

St.-Germain assumed a grave expression. "Did this Marquis Balletti have a bad reputation?" he asked.

"On the contrary," replied the Comtesse, "he was in very
good society."

The Comte shrugged his shoulders expressively saying:
"Well, as no one complains of him, I adopt him willingly as
my grandfather."

The Comtesse d'Adhemar was present during the entire
conversation and vouches for its accuracy in every detail.

Madame du Hausset, femme de chambre to Madame de
Pompadour, writes at some length of the astonishing man who
often called upon her mistress. She records a conversation
which took place between la Pompadour and St.-Germain:

"It is true, Madame, that I knew Madame de Gergy long
ago," the Comte affirmed quietly.

"But, according to that," replied the Marquise, "you must
now be more than a hundred years old."

"That is not impossible," enigmatically returned the Comte
with a slight smile, "but I admit that it is more possible that
this lady, for whom I have infinite respect, talks nonsense."

It was answers such as this which led Gustave Bord to write
of St.-Germain that, "he allows a certain mystery to hover

about him, a mystery which awakens curiosity and sympathy. Being a virtuoso in the art of misleading he says nothing that is untrue. * * * He has the rare gift of remaining silent and profiting by it." (See La Franc-Maconnerie en France, etc.)

But to return to Madame du Hausset's story. "You gave Madame de Gergy," pressed la Pompadour, "an elixir surprising in its effects; she pretends that for a long while she appeared to be no older than twenty-four. Why should you not give some to the king?"

St. Germain allowed an expression feigning terror to spread over his face, "Ah! Madame, I should be mad indeed to take it into my head to give the king an unknown drug!"

The Comte was on very friendly terms with Louis XV with whom he had long discussions on the subject of precious stones, their manufacture and purification. Louis was amused and thrilled by turns. Never before had so extraordinary a person trod the sacred precincts of Versailles. The whole court was topsy-turvy and miracles were the order of the day. Courtiers of depleted fortunes envisioned the magical multiplication of their gold and grandames of uncertain age had dreams of youth and favor restored by the mystery man's fabled elixirs. It is easy to understand how so fascinating a character could relieve the boredom of a king who had spent his life a martyr to royal fashions and was deprived by his position of the pleasure of honest work. Then, again, rulers become victims to the fads of the moment and Louis himself was dabbling in alchemy and other occult arts. True, the king was only a dilettante whose will was not strong enough to bind him to any lasting purpose, but St.-Germain appealed to several qualities in the royal nature. The Comte's fund of knowledge, the skill with which he assembled his facts to the amusement and edification of his audiences, the mystery which surrounded his appearances and disappearances, his consummate skill both as a critic and technician in the arts and sciences, to say nothing of his jewels and wealth, endeared him to the king. Had Louis but profited by the wisdom and prophetic warnings of the mysterious Comte, the Reign of Terror might have been averted. St.-Germain was ever the patron, never the patronized. Louis had found the diplomat in whom there was no guile.

De Pompadour writes, "He enriched the cabinet of the king by his pictures by Velasquez and Murillo, and he presented to the Marquise the most precious and priceless gems. For this singular man passed for being fabulously rich and he distributed diamonds and jewels with astonishing liberality."

Not the least admirable evidence of the Comte's genius was his penetrating grasp of the political situation of Europe and the consummate skill with which he parried the thrusts of his diplomatic adversaries. At all times he bore credentials which gave him entry to the most exclusive circles of European nobility. During the reign of Peter the Great, M. de St.-Germain was in Russia, and between the years 1737 and 1742 in the court of the Shah of Persia as an honored guest. On the subject of his wanderings, Una Birch writes: "The travels of the Comte de Saint-Germain covered a long period of years and a great range of countries. From Persia to France and from Calcutta to Rome he was known and respected. Horace Walpole spoke with him in London in 1745; Clive knew him in India in 1756; Madame d'Adhemar alleges that she met him in Paris in 1789, five years after his supposed death; while other persons pretend to have held conversations with him in the early nineteenth century. He was on familiar and intimate terms with the crowned heads of Europe and the honoured friend of many distinguished persons of all nationalities. He is even mentioned in the memoirs and letters of the day, and always as a man of mystery. Frederick the Great, Voltaire, Madame de Pompadour, Rousseau, Chatham, and Walpole, all of whom knew him personally, rivalled each other in curiosity as to his origin. During the many decades in which he was before the world, however, no one succeeded in discovering why he appeared as a Jacobite agent in London, as a conspirator in Petersburg, as an alchemist and connoisseur of pictures in Paris, or as a Russian general at Naples. * * * Now and again the curtain which shrouds his actions is drawn aside, and we are permitted to see him fiddling in the music room at Versailles, gossiping with Horace Walpole in London, sitting in Frederick the Great's library at Berlin, or conducting illuminist meetings in caverns by the Rhine." (See *The Nineteenth Century,* January, 1908.)

In the realm of music St.-Germain was equally a master. While at Versailles he gave concerts on the violin and on at least one occasion during an eventful life he conducted a symphony orchestra without a score. In Paris St.-Germain was the diplomat and the alchemist, in London he was the musician. "He left a musical record behind him to remind English people of his sojourn in this country. Many of his compositions were published by Walsh, in Catherine Street, Strand, and his earliest English song, *Oh, wouldst thou know what sacred charms,* came out while he was still on his first visit to London; but on quitting this city he entrusted certain other settings of words to Walsh, such as *Jove, when he saw,* and the arias out of his little opera *L'Inconstanza Delusa,* both of which compositions were published during his absence from England. When he returned, in 1760, he gave the world a great many new songs, followed in 1780 by a set of solos for the violin. He was an industrious and capable artist, and attracted a great deal of fashionable attention to himself both as composer and executant."

An old English newspaper, *The London Chronicle*, for June, 1760, contains the following anecdote: "With regard to music, he not only played but composed; and both in high taste. Nay, his very ideas were accommodated to the art; and in those occurrences which had no relation to music he found means to express himself in figurative terms deduced from this science. There could not be a more artful way of showing his attention to the subject. I remember an incident which impressed it strongly upon my memory. I had the honour to be at an assembly of Lady . . . . . , who to many other good and great accomplishments added a taste for music so delicate that she was made a judge in the dispute of masters. This stranger was to be of the party; and towards evening he came in his usual free and polite manner, but with more hurry than was customary, and with his fingers stopped in his ears. I can conceive easily that in most men this would have been a very ungraceful attitude, and I am afraid it would have been construed into an ungenteel entrance; but he had a manner that made everything agreeable. They had been emptying a cartload of stones just at the door, to mend the pavement; he threw himself into a chair and, when the lady asked what was the matter, he pointed to the place and said, 'I am stunned with a whole cartload of discords.' "

In his memoirs the Italian adventurer Jacques de Casanova de Seingalt makes numerous references to his acquaintance with St.-Germain. Casanova grudgingly admits that the Comte was an adept at magical arts, a skilled linguist, musician and chemist who won the favor of the ladies of the French court not only by the general air of mystery surrounding him but his surpassing skill in preparing pigments and cosmetics by which he preserved for them at least a shadow of swift departing youth.

Casanova describes a meeting with St.-Germain which occurred in Belgium under most unusual circumstances. Having arrived at Tournay, Casanova was surprised to see some grooms walking spirited horses up and down. He asked to whom the fine animals belonged and was told: "To the Comte de St.-Germain, the adept, who has been here a month and never goes out. Everybody who passes through the place wants to see him, but he makes himself visible to no one." This was sufficient to excite the curiosity of Casanova, who wrote requesting an appointment. He received the following answer: "The gravity of my occupation compels me to exclude everyone, but in your case I will make an exception. Come whenever you like and you will be shown in. You need not mention my name nor your own. I do not ask you to share my repast, for my food is not suitable to others, to you least of all, if your appetite is what it used to be." At nine o'clock Casanova called and found that the Comte had grown a beard two inches long. In discussion with Casanova, the Comte explained his presence in Belgium by stating that Count Cobenzl, the Austrian ambassador at Brussels, desired to establish a hat factory and that he was taking care of the details. Upon his telling St.-Germain that he was suffering from an acute disease, the Comte invited Casanova to remain for treatment, saying that he would prepare fifteen pills which in three days would restore the Italian to perfect health.

Casanova writes: "Then he showed me his magistrum, which he called *athoeter*. It was a white liquid contained in a well stopped phial. He told me that this liquid was the universal spirit of Nature and that if the wax of the stopper was pricked even so slightly, the whole of the contents would dis-appear. I begged him to make the experiment. He thereupon gave me the phial and the pin and I myself pricked the wax, when, lo, the phial was empty." Casanova, being somewhat of a rogue himself, doubted all other men. Therefore, he refused to permit St.-Germain to treat his malady. He could not deny, however, that St.-Germain was a chemist of extraordinary skill, whose accomplishments were astonishing if not practical. The adept refused to disclose the purpose for which these chemical experiments were intended, maintaining that such information could not be communicated.

Casanova further records an incident in which St.-Germain changed a twelve-sols piece into a pure gold coin. Being a doubting Thomas, Casanova declared that he felt sure that St.-Germain had substituted one coin for another. He intimated so to the Comte who replied: "Those who are capable of entertaining doubts of my work are not worthy to speak to me," and bowed the Italian out. This was the last time Casanova ever saw St.-Germain.

There is other evidence that the celebrated Comte possessed the alchemical powder by which it is possible to transmute base metals into gold. He actually performed this feat on at least two occasions, as attested by the writings of contemporaries. The Marquis de Valbelle, visiting St.-Germain in his laboratory, found the alchemist busy with his furnaces. He asked the Marquis for a silver six-franc piece and, covering it with a black substance, exposed it to the heat of a small flame or furnace. M. de Valbelle saw the coin change color until it turned a bright red. Some minutes after, when it had cooled a little, the adept took it out of the cooling vessel and returned it to the Marquis. The piece was no longer of silver but of the purest gold. Transmutation had been complete. The Comtesse d'Adhemar had possession of this coin until 1786 when it was stolen from her secretary.

One author tells us that, "Saint-Germain always attributed his knowledge of occult chemistry to his sojourn in Asia. In 1755 he went to the East again for the second time, and writing to Count von Lamberg he said, 'I am indebted for my knowledge of melting jewels to my second journey to India.' "

There are too many authentic cases of metallic transmutations to condemn St.-Germain as a charlatan for such a feat. The Leopold-Hoffman medal, still in the possession of that family, is the most outstanding example of the transmutation of metals ever recorded. Two-thirds of this medal was transformed into gold by the monk Wenzel Seiler, leaving the balance silver which was its original state. In this case fraud was impossible as there was but one copy of the medal extant. The ease with which we condemn as fraudulent and unreal anything which transcends our understanding has brought unjustified calumny upon the names and memories of many illustrious persons.

The popular belief that Comte de St.-Germain was merely an adventurer is not supported by even a shred of evidence. He was never detected in any subterfuge nor did he betray, even to the slightest degree, the confidence entrusted to him. His great wealth—for he was always amply supplied with this world's goods—was not extracted from those with whom he came in contact. Every effort to determine the source and size of his fortune was fruitless. He made use of neither bank nor banker yet moved in a sphere of unlimited credit, which was neither questioned by others nor abused by himself.

Referring to the attacks upon his character, H. P. Blavatsky wrote in *The Theosophist* of March, 1881: "Do charlatans enjoy the confidence and admiration of the cleverest statesmen and nobles of Europe for long years, and not even at their deaths show in one thing that they were undeserving? Some encyclopaedists (see *New American Cyclopedia,* xiv. 266) say: 'He is supposed *to have been employed during the greater part of his life as a spy* at the courts at which he resided.' But upon what evidence is this supposition based? Has anyone found it in any of the state papers in the secret archives of either of those courts? Not one word, not one shred of fact to build this base calumny upon, has ever been found. It is simply a malicious lie. The treatment this great man, this pupil of Indian and Egyptian hierophants, this proficient in the secret wisdom of the East, has had from Western writers, is a stigma upon human nature."

Nothing is known concerning the source of the Comte de St.-Germain's occult knowledge. Most certainly he not only intimated his possession of a vast amount of wisdom but he also gave many examples in support of his claims. When asked once about himself, he replied that his father was the Secret Doctrine and his mother the Mysteries. St.-Germain was thoroughly conversant with the principles of Oriental esotericism. He practiced the Eastern system of meditation and concentration, upon several occasions having been seen seated with his feet crossed and hands folded in the posture of a Hindu Buddha. He had a retreat in the heart of the Himalayas to which he retired periodically from the world. On one occasion he declared that he would remain in India for eighty-five years and then return to the scene of his European labors. At various times he admitted that he was obeying the orders of a power higher and greater than himself. What he did not say was that this superior power was the Mystery School which had sent him into the world to accomplish a definite mission. The Comte de St.-Germain and Sir Francis Bacon are the two greatest emissaries sent into the world by the Secret Brotherhood in the last thousand years.

The principles disseminated by the Comte de St.-Germain

were undoubtedly Rosicrucian in orgin and permeated with the doctrines of the Gnostics. The Comte was the moving spirit of Rosicrucianism during the eighteenth century—possibly the actual head of that order—and is suspected of being the great power behind the French Revolution. There is also reason to believe that Lord Bulwer-Lytton's famous novel, *Zanoni,* is actually concerned with the life and activities of St.-Germain. He is generally regarded as an important figure in the early activities of the Freemasons. Repeated efforts, however, probably with an ulterior motive, have been made to discredit his Masonic affiliations. Maags of London are offering for sale a Masonic minute book in which the signatures of both Comte de St.-Germain and the Marquis de Lafayette appear. It will yet be established beyond all doubt that the Comte was both a Mason and a Templar; in fact, the memoirs of Cagliostro contain a direct statement of his own initiation into the order of the Knights Templars at the hands of St.-Germain. Many of the illustrious personages with whom the Comte associated were high Masons, and sufficient memoranda have been preserved concerning the discussions which they held to prove that he was a master of Freemasonic lore.

Madame d'Adhemar who has preserved so many anecdotes of the life of the "wonder man," copied from one of St.-Germain's letters the following prophetic verses pertaining to the downfall of the French Empire:

"The time is fast approaching when imprudent France,
Surrounded by misfortune she might have spared herself,
Will cali to mind such hell as Dante painted.
Falling shall we see sceptre, censer, scales,
Towers and escutcheons, even the white flag.
Great streams of blood are flowing in each town;
Sobs only do I hear, and exiles see.

On all sides civil discord loudly roars
And uttering cries, on all sides virtue flees
As from the Assembly votes of death arise.
Great God, who can reply to murderous judges?
And on what brows august I see swords descend!

Marie Antoinette was much disturbed by the direful nature
of the prophecies and questioned Madame d'Adhemar as to
her opinion of their significance. Madame replied, "They are
dismaying but certainly they cannot affect Your Majesty."

Madame d'Adhemar also recounts a dramatic incident.
St.-Germain offered to meet the good lady at the Church of
the *Recollets* about the hour of the eight o'clock mass. Madame went to the appointed place in her sedan chair and recorded the following conversation between herself and the
mysterious adept:

St.-Germain: I am Cassandra, prophet of evil . . . Madame,
he who sows the wind reaps the whirlwind . . . I can do
nothing; *my hands are tied by a stronger than myself.*

Madame: Will you see the Queen?

St.-Germain: No; she is doomed.

Madame: Doomed to what?

St.-Germain: Death.

Madame: And you—you too?

St.-Germain: Yes—like Cazotte—Return to the Palace; tell
the Queen to take heed of herself, that this day will be
fatal to her . . .

Madame: But M. de Lafayette . . .

St.-Germain: A balloon inflated with wind. Even now, they

are settling what to do with him, whether he shall be instrument or victim; by noon all will be decided ... The hour of repose is past, and the decrees of Providence must be fulfilled.

Madame: What do they want?

St.-Germain: The complete ruin of the Bourbons. They will expel them from all the thrones they occupy and in less than a century they will return in all their different branches to the rank of simple private individuals. France as Kingdom, Republic, Empire, and mixed Government will be tormented, agitated, torn. From the hands of class tyrants she will pass to those who are ambitious and without merit.

Comte de St.-Germain disappeared from the stage of French mysticism as suddenly and inexplicably as he had appeared. Nothing is known with positive certainty after that disappearance. It is claimed by transcendentalists that he retired into the secret order which had sent him into the world for a particular and peculiar purpose. Having accomplished this mission, he vanished. From the *Memoirs de Mon Temps* of Charles, Landgrave of Hesse Cassel, we gain several particulars concerning the last years before the death or disappearance of the Hungarian adept. Charles was deeply interested in occult and Masonic mysteries, and a secret society, of which he was the moving spirit, held occasional meetings upon his estate. The purposes of this organization were similar to, if not identical with, Cagliostro's Egyptian Rite. In fact, after studying the fragments left by the Landgrave, Cagliostro's contention that he was initiated into Egyptian Masonry by St.-Germain is proved beyond a reasonable doubt. The "Wonder Man" attended at least some of these secret meetings and of all whom he met and knew during life, he confided more in Prince

Charles than in any other man. The last years of St.-Germain's known life were therefore divided between his experimental research work in alchemy with Charles of Hesse and the Mystery School at Louisenlund, in Schleswig, where philosophic and political problems were under discussion.

According to popular tradition, it was on the estate of Prince Charles that St.-Germain finally died at a date given out as 1784. The strange circumstances connected with his passing lead us to suspect that it was a mock funeral similar to that given the English adept, Lord Bacon. It has been noted that, "Great uncertainty and vagueness surround his latter days, for no confidence can be reposed in the announcement of the death of one illuminate by another, for, as is well known, all means to secure the end were in their code justifiable, and it may have been to the interest of the society that St.-Germain should have been thought dead."

H. P. Blavatsky remarks: "Is it not absurd to suppose that if he really died at the time and place mentioned, he would have been laid in the ground without the pomp and ceremony, the official supervision, the police registration which attend the funerals of men of his rank and notoriety? Where are these data? He passed out of public sight more than a century ago, yet no memoirs contain them. A man who so lived in the full blaze of publicity could not have vanished, *if he really died then and there,* and left no trace behind. Moreover, to this negative we have the alleged positive proof that he was living several years after 1784. He is said to have had a most important private conference with the Empress of Russia in 1785 or 1786 and to have appeared to the Princess de Lambelle when she stood before the tribunal, a few minutes before she was struck down with a billet, and a butcher-boy cut off her head; and to Jeanne Dubarry, the mistress of Louis XV as she waited on her scaffold at Paris the stroke of the guillotine in the Days of Terror of 1793."

It should be added that the Comte de Chalons, on his return from an embassy to Venice in 1788, said that he had conversed with the Comte de St.-Germain in the square at St. Mark's the evening before his departure. The Comtesse d' Adhemar also saw and talked with him after his presumed decease, and the *Encyclopedia Britannica* notes that he is said to have attended a Masonic conference several years after his death had been reported. In concluding an article on the identity of the inscrutable Comte, Andrew Lang writes: "Did Saint-Germain really die in the palace of Prince Charles of Hesse about 1780-85? Did he, on the other hand, escape from the French prison where Grosley thought he saw him, during the Revolution? Was he known to Lord Lytton about 1860? * * * Is he the mysterious Muscovite adviser of the Dalai Lama? Who knows? He is a will-o'-the wisp of the memoir writers of the eighteenth century." (See *Historical Mysteries*.)

The true purpose for which St.-Germain labored must remain obscure until the dawn of a new era. Homer refers to the Golden Chain by which the gods conspired to bind the earth to the pinnacle of Olympus. In each age there appear some few persons whose words and actions demonstrate clearly that they are of an order different from the rest of society. Humanity is guided over critical periods in the development of civilization by mysterious forces such as were personified in the eccentric Comte de St.-Germain. Until we recognize the reality of the occult forces at work in every-day life, we cannot grasp the significance of either the man or his work. To the wise, St.-Germain is no wonder—to those who are limited by belief in the inevitability of the commonplace, he is indeed a magician, defying the laws of nature and violating the smugness of the pseudo-learned.

THE RAREST OF OCCULT MANUSCRIPTS

O F the utmost significance to all students of Free-masonry and the occult sciences is this unique manuscript *La Très Sainte Trinosophie*. Not only is it the only known mystical writing of the Comte de St.-Germain, but it is one of the most extraordinary documents relating to the Hermetic sciences ever compiled.* Though the libraries of European Rosicrucians and Cabbalists contain many rare treasures of ancient philosophical lore, it is extremely doubtful if any of them include a treatise of greater value or significance. There is a persistent rumor that St.-Germain possessed a magnificent library, and that he prepared a number of manuscripts on the secret sciences for the use of his disciples. At the time of his death . . . or disappearance . . . these books and papers vanished, probably into the archives of his society, and no trustworthy information is now available as to their whereabouts.

The mysterious Comte is known to have possessed at one time a copy of the Vatican manuscript of the Cabbala, a work of extraordinary profundity setting forth the doctrines of the Luciferians, Lucianists and the Gnostics. The second volume of *The Secret Doctrine* by H. P. Blavatsky (pp. 582-83 of the

* Since this work was first published another manuscript by St. Germain has been found. It is in my possession and will soon be published. (M. P. H.)

original edition) contains two quotations from a manuscript "supposed to be by the Comte St.-Germain." The parts of the paragraphs attributed to the Hungarian adept are not clearly indicated, but as the entire text deals with the significance of numbers, it is reasonable to infer that his commentaries are mystical interpretations of the numerals 4 and 5. Both paragraphs are in substance similar to the *Puissance des nombres d'après Pythagore* by Jean Marie Ragon. The Mahatma Koot Hoomi mentions a "ciphered MS." by St.-Germain which remained with his staunch friend and patron the benevolent Prince Charles of Hesse-Cassel (See *Mahatma Letters to A. P. Sinnett*). Comparatively unimportant references to St.-Germain, and wild speculations concerning his origin and the purpose of his European activities, are available in abundance, but the most exhaustive search of the work of eighteenth century memoir writers for information regarding the Masonic and metaphysical doctrines which he promulgated has proved fruitless. So far as it has been possible to ascertain, the present translation and publication of *La Très Sainte Trinosophie* affords the first opportunity to possess a work setting forth . . . in the usual veiled and symbolic manner . . . the esoteric doctrines of St.-Germain, and his associates.

La Très Sainte Trinosophie is MS. No. 2400 in the French Library at Troyes. The work is of no great length, consisting of ninety-six leaves written upon one side only. The calligraphy is excellent. Although somewhat irregular in spelling and accenting, the French is scholarly and dramatic, and the text is embellished with numerous figures, well drawn and brilliantly colored. In addition to the full-page drawings there are small symbols at the beginning and end of each of the sections. Throughout the French text there are scattered letters, words, and phrases in several ancient languages. There are also magical symbols, figures resembling Egyptian hieroglyphics, and a few words in character resembling cuneiform. At the end of the manuscript are a number of leaves written in arbitrary ciphers, possibly the code used by St.-Germain's secret society. The work was probably executed in the latter part of the eighteenth century, though most of the material belongs to a considerably earlier period.

As to the history of this remarkable manuscript, too little, unfortunately, is known. The illustrious Freemasonic martyr, the Comte Allesandro Cagliostro, carried this book amongst others with him on his ill-fated journey to Rome. After Cagliostro's incarceration in the Castle San Leo, all trace of the manuscript was temporarily lost. Eventually Cagliostro's literary effects came into the possession of a general in Napoleon's army, and upon this officer's death *La Très Sainte Trinosophie* was bought at a nominal price by the Bibliotheque de Troyes. In his *Musée des Sorciers,* Grillot de Givry adds somewhat to the meager notes concerning the manuscript. He states that the volume was bought at the sale of Messena's effects; that in the front of the book is a note by a philosopher who signs himself "I.B.C. Philotaume" who states that the manuscript belonged to him and is the sole existing copy of the famous *Trinosophie* of the Comte de St.-Germain, the original of which the Comte himself destroyed on one of his journeys. The note then adds that Cagliostro had owned the volume, but that the Inquisition had seized it in Rome when he was arrested at the end of 1789. (It should be remembered that Cagliostro and his wife had visited St.-Germain at a castle in Holstein). De Givry sums up the contents of *La Très Sainte Trinosophie* as "Cabbalized alchemy" and describes St.-Germain as "one of the enigmatic personages of the eighteenth century . . . an alchemist and man of the world who passed through the drawing rooms of all Europe and ended by falling into the dungeons of the Inquisition at Rome, if the manuscript is to be believed."

The title of the manuscript, *La Très Sainte Trinosophie,* translated into English means "The Most Holy Trinosophia" or "The Most Holy Three-fold Wisdom." The title itself opens a considerable field of speculation. Is there any connection between *La Très Sainte Trinosophie* and the Masonic brother-hood of *Les Trinosophists* which was founded in 1805 by the distinguished Belgian Freemason and mystic Jean Marie Ragon, already referred to? The knowledge of occultism posses-sed by Ragon is mentioned in terms of the highest respect by H. P. Blavatsky who says of him that "for fifty years he studied the ancient mysteries wherever he could find accounts of them." Is it not possible that Ragon as a young man either knew St.-Germain or contacted his secret society? Ragon was termed by his contemporaries "the most learned Mason of the nineteenth century." In 1818, before the Lodge of *Les Trin-osophists,* he delivered a course of lectures on ancient and mod-ern initiation which he repeated at the request of that lodge in 1841. These lectures were published under the title *Cours Philosophique et Interprétatif des Initiations Anciennes et Modernes.* In 1853 Ragon published his most important work *Orthodoxie Maconnique.* Ragon died in Paris about 1866 and two years later his unfinished manuscripts were purchased from his heirs by the Grand Orient of France for one thousand francs. A high Mason told Madam Blavatsky that Ragon had corresponded for years with two Orientalists in Syria and Egypt, one of whom was a Copt gentleman.

Ragon defined the Lodge of the *Trinosophists* as "those who study three sciences." Madam Blavatsky writes: "It is on the occult properties of the three equal lines or sides of the Triangle that Ragon based his studies and founded the famous Masonic Society of the *Trinosophists*." Ragon describes the symbolism of the triangle in substance as follows: The first side or line represents the mineral kingdom which is the proper study for Apprentices; the second line represents the vegetable kingdom which the Companions should learn to understand because in this kingdom generation of bodies begins; the third line represents the animal kingdom from the exploration of which the Master Mason must complete his education. It has been said of the Lodge of the *Trinosophists* that "it was at one time the most intelligent society of Freemasons ever known. It adhered to the ancient Landmarks but gave clearer and more satisfactory interpretations to the symbols of Freemasonry than are afforded in the symbolical Lodges." It practiced five degrees. In the Third, candidates for initiation received a philosophic and astronomic explanation of the Hiramic Legend.

The Egyptianized interpretation of Freemasonic symbolism which is so evident in the writings of Ragon and other French Masonic scholars of the same period (such as Court de Gebelin and Alexandre Lenoir) is also present in the figures and text of the St.-Germain manuscript. In his comments on the Rite of Misraim, called the Egyptian Rite, Ragon distinguishes 90 degrees of Masonic Mysteries. The 1st to 33rd degrees he terms symbolic; the 34th to 66th degrees, philosophic; the 67th to 77th, mystic; and the 78th to 90th, Cabbalistic. The Egyptian Freemasonry of Cagliostro may also have been derived from St.-Germain or from some common body of Illuminists of whom St.-Germain was the moving spirit. Cagliostro's memoirs contain a direct statement of his initiation into the Order of Knights Templars at the hands of St.-Germain. De Luchet gives what a modern writer on Cagliostro calls a fantastic account of the visit paid by Allesandro and his wife the Comtesse Felicitas to St.-Germain in Germany, and their subsequent initiation by him into the sect of the Rosicrucians—of which he was the Grand Master or chief. There is nothing improbable in the assumption that Cagliostro secured *La Très Sainte Trinosophie* from St.-Germain and that the manuscript is in every respect an authentic ritual of this society.

The word *Trinosophie* quite properly infers a triple meaning to the contents of the book, in other words that its meaning should be interpreted with the aid of three keys. From the symbolism it seems that one of these keys is alchemy, or soul-chemistry; another Essenian Cabbalism; and the third Alexandrian Hermetism, the mysticism of the later Egyptians. From such fragments of the Rosicrucian lore as now exist, it is evident that the Brethren of the Rose Cross were especially addicted to these three forms of the ancient wisdom, and chose the symbols of these schools as the vehicles of their ideas.

The technical task of decoding the hieroglyphics occurring throughout *La Très Sainte Trinosophie* was assigned to Dr. Edward C. Getsinger, an eminent authority on ancient alphabets and languages, who is now engaged in the decoding of the primitive ciphers in the Book of Genesis. A few words from his notes will give an idea of the difficulties involved in decoding:

"Archaic writings are usually in one system of letters or characters, but those among the ancients who were in possession of the sacred mysteries of life and certain secret astronomical cycles never trusted this knowledge to ordinary writing, but devised secret codes by which they concealed their wisdom from the unworthy. Each of these communities or brotherhoods of the enlightened devised its own code. About 3000 B. C. only the Initiates and their scribes could read and write. At that period the simpler methods of concealment were in vogue, one of which was to drop certain letters from words in such a manner that the remaining letters still formed a word which, however, conveyed an entirely different sense. As ages progressed other systems were invented, until human ingenuity was taxed to the utmost in an endeavor to conceal and yet perpetuate sacred knowledge.

"In order to decipher ancient writings of a religious or philosophic nature, it is first necessary to discover the code or method of concealment used by the scribe. In all my twenty years of experience as a reader of archaic writings I have never encountered such ingenious codes and methods of concealment as are found in this manuscript. In only a few instances are complete phrases written in the same alphabet; usually two or three forms of writing are employed, with letters written upside down, reversed, or with the text written backwards. Vowels are often omitted, and at times several letters are missing with merely dots to indicate their number. Every combination of hieroglyphics seemed hopeless at the beginning, yet, after hours of alphabetic dissection, one familiar word would appear. This gave a clue as to the language used, and established a place where word combination might begin, and then a sentence would gradually unfold.

"The various texts are written in Chaldean Hebrew, Ionic Greek, Arabic, Syriac, cuneiform, Greek hieroglyphics, and ideographs. The keynote throughout this material is that of the approach of the age when the Leg of the Grand Man and the Waterman of the Zodiac shall meet in conjunction at the equinox and end a grand 400,000-year cycle. This points to a culmination of eons, as mentioned in the Apocalypse: "Behold! I make a new heaven and a new earth," meaning a series of new cycles and a new humanity.

"The personage who gathered the material in this manuscript was indeed one whose spiritual understanding might be envied. He found these various texts in different parts of Europe, no doubt, and that he had a true knowledge of their import is proved by the fact that he attempted to conceal some forty fragmentary ancient texts by scattering them within the lines of his own writing. Yet his own text does not appear to have any connection with these ancient writings. If a decipherer were to be guided by what this eminent scholar wrote he would never decipher the mystery concealed within the cryptic words. There is a marvelous spiritual story written by this savant, and a more wonderful one he interwove within the pattern of his own narrative. The result is a story within a story."

The reprint of the French text of *La Très Sainte Trinosopie* is a complete photostatic facsimile of the original work in the French Library at Troyes. The present manuscript is undoubtedly a copy, as "Philotaume" stated. The archaic characters and the hieroglyphics reveal minor imperfections of formation due to the copyist being unfamiliar with the alphabets employed.

The considerable extent of the notes and commentaries has made it advisable to place them together at the end of the work rather than break up the continuity of the text by over-frequent interpolations.

La Très Sainte Trinosophie is not a manuscript for the tyro. Only deep study and consideration will unravel the complicated skein of its symbolism. Although the text matter is treated with the utmost simplicity, every line is a profound enigma. Careful perusal of the book, and meditation upon its contents, will convince the scholar that it has been well designated "the most precious known manuscript of occultism."

ENGLISH TRANSLATION OF
THE
MOST HOLY TRINOSOPHIA

LE COMTE DE St. GERMAIN
CÉLÈBRE ALCHIMISTE.

Ainsi que Prométhée il déroba le feu
Par qui le Monde exife, et par qui tout respire,
La Nature à sa voix obéit et se meut
S'il n'est pas Dieu lui-même un Dieu puissant l'inspire.

THE MOST HOLY TRINOSOPHIA

SECTION ONE

I T *is in the retreat of criminals in the dungeons of the Inquisition that your friend writes these lines which are to serve for your instruction. At the thought of the inestimable advantages which this document of friendship will procure for you, the horrors of a long and little deserved captivity seem to be mitigated . . . It gives me pleasure to think that while surrounded by guards and encumbered by chains, a slave may still be able to raise his friend above the mighty, the monarchs who rule this place of exile.*

My dear Philochatus, you are about to penetrate into the sanctuary of the sublime sciences; my hand is about to raise for you the impenetrable veil which hides from the eyes of common men the tabernacle, the sanctuary wherein the Eternal has lodged the secrets of nature, kept for a few that are privileged, the few Elect whom His omnipotence created that they may SEE, and seeing, may soar after Him in the vast expanse of His Glory and deflect upon mankind one of the Rays that shine round about His golden Throne.

If your friend's example proves a salutary lesson for you, I shall bless the long years of tribulation which the wicked have made me suffer.

Two stumbling blocks equally dangerous will constantly present themselves to you. One of them would outrage the sacred rights of every individual. It is Misuse of the power which God will have entrusted to you; the other, which would bring ruin upon you, is Indiscretion . . . Both are born of the same mother, both owe their existence to pride. Human frailty nourishes them; they are blind; their mother leads them. With her aid these two Monsters carry their foul breath even into the hearts of the Lord's Elect. Woe unto him who misuses the gifts of heaven in order to serve his passions. The Almighty Hand that made the elements subject to him, would break him like a fragile reed. An eternity of torments could hardly expiate his crime. The Infernal Spirits would smile with contempt at the tears of the one whose menacing voice had so often made them tremble in the bosom of their fiery depths.

It is not for you, Philochatus, that I sketch this dreadful picture. The friend of humanity will never become its persecutor . . . The precipice, my son, which I fear for you, is Indiscretion, the imperious craving to inspire astonishment and admiration. God leaves to men the task of punishing the imprudent minister who permits the eye of the profane to look into the mysterious sanctuary. Oh Philochatus, may my sorrows be ever present in your mind. I, too, have known happiness, was showered with the blessings of heaven and surrounded by power such as the human mind cannot conceive. Commanding the genii that guide the world, happy in the happiness that I created, I enjoyed within the bosom of an adored family the felicity which the Eternal accords to His beloved children. One moment destroyed everything. I spoke, and it all vanished like a cloud. O my son, follow not in my steps . . . Let no vain desire to shine before men bring you, too, to disaster . . . Think of me, your friend, writing to you from this dungeon, my body broken by torture! Remember, Philochatus, that the hand which traces these characters bears the marks of the chains which weigh it down. God has punished me, but what have I done to the cruel men that persecute me? What right have they to interrogate the minister of the Eternal? They ask me what are the proofs of my mission. My witnesses are prodigies, and my virtues are my defenders—a clean life, a pure heart. But what am I saying! Have I still the right to complain? I spoke, and the Lord delivered me, deprived of strength and power, to the furies of greedy fanaticism. The arm which once could overthrow an army can today hardly lift the chains that weigh it down.

I wander. I should give thanks to eternal Justice . . . The avenging God has pardoned His repentant child. An aerial spirit has entered through the walls which separate me from the world; he has shown himself to me resplendent with light and has determined the duration of my captivity. Within two years my sufferings will end. My torturers upon entering my cell will find it empty and, soon purified by the four elements, pure as the genius of fire, I shall resume the glorious station to which Divine goodness has raised me. But how distant as yet is this time! How long two years seem to one who spends them in suffering and humiliation. Not content with making me undergo the most horrible agony, my oppressors, to torture me further have devised still surer, still more revolting means. They have brought infamy on my head, have made my name a thing of disgrace. The children of men recoil in terror when by chance they approach the walls of my prison; they fear lest some deadly vapour escape through the narrow slit that reluctantly admits a ray of light to my cell. That, O Philochatus, is the cruelest of all blows that they could bear down upon me.

I know not whether I shall be able to get this document into your hands . . . I judge the difficulty I shall have in con-

triving for it a way out of this place of torture by those I have had in order to write it. Deprived of all help, I myself have composed the agents I needed. The flame of my lamp, some coins, and a few chemical substances overlooked by the scrutinizing eyes of my tormentors have yielded the colours which adorn this fruit of a prisoner's leisure.

Profit by the instructions of your unhappy friend! They are so clear that danger exists for them to fall into hands other than yours . . . Remember only that all of it is to serve you . . . an obscure line, an omitted character would prevent your lifting the veil which the hand of the Creator has placed over the Sphinx.

Adieu, Philochatus! Do not mourn me. The clemency of the Eternal equals His justice. At the first mysterious assembly you will see your friend again. I salute you in the name of God. Soon I shall give the kiss of peace to my brother.

SECTION TWO

I*T was night. The moon, veiled by dark clouds, cast but an uncertain light on the crags of lava that hemmed in the Solfatara. My head covered with the linen veil, holding in my hands the golden bough, I advanced without fear toward the spot where I had been ordered to pass the night. I was groping over hot sand which I felt give way under my every step. The clouds gathered overhead. Lightning flashed through the night and gave to the flames of the volcano a bloodlike appearance. At last I arrived and found an iron altar where I placed the mysterious bough . . . I pronounce the formidable words . . . instantly the earth trembles under my feet, thunder peals . . . Vesuvius roars in answer to the repeated strokes; its fires join the fires of lightning . . . The choirs of the genii rise into the air and make the echoes repeat the praises of the Creator . . . The hallowed bough which I had placed on the triangular altar suddenly is ablaze. A thick smoke envelops me. I cease to see. Wrapped in darkness, I seemed to descend into an abyss. I know not how long I remained in that situation. When I opened my eyes I vainly looked for the objects which had surrounded me a little time ago. The altar, Vesuvius, the country round Naples had vanished far from my sight. I was in a vast cavern, alone, far away from the whole world . . . Near by me lay a long, white robe; its loosely woven tissue seemed to me to be of linen. On a granite boulder stood a copper lamp upon a black table covered with Greek words indicating* *the way I was to follow. I took the lamp, and after having put on the robe I entered a narrow passage the walls of which were covered with black marble . . . It was three miles long and my steps resounded fearfully under its silent vault. At last I found a door that opened on a flight of steps which I descended. After having walked a long time I seemed to see a wandering light before me. I hid my lamp and fixed my eyes on the object which I beheld. It dissipated, vanishing like a shadow.*

Without reproach of the past, without fear of the future, I went on. The way became increasingly difficult . . . always confined within galleries composed of black stone blocks . . . I did not dare to guess at the length of my underground travel. At last, after a long, long march I came to a square chamber. A door in the middle of each of its four sides opened; they were of different colours, and each door was placed at one of the four cardinal points. I entered through the north door which was black; the opposite one was red; the door to the east was blue and the one facing it was of dazzling white . . . In the middle of this chamber was a square mass; on its center shone a crystal star. On the north side was a painting representing a woman naked to the waist; a black drapery fell over her knees and two silver bands adorned her garment. In her hand was a rod which she placed against the forehead of a man facing her across a table which stood on a single support and bore a cup and a lance-head. A sudden flame rose from the ground and seemed to turn toward the man. An inscription explained this picture; another indicated the means I was to employ in order to leave this chamber.

After having contemplated the picture and the star I was about to pass through the red door when, turning on its hinges with terrific noise, it closed before me. I made the same at-

tempt with the door of sky-blue colour; it did not close but a sudden noise induced me to turn my head. I saw the star flicker, rise from its place, revolve, then dart rapidly through the opening of the white door. I followed it at once.

SECTION THREE

A STRONG wind arose and I had difficulty in keeping my lamp alight. At last I saw a white marble platform to which I mounted by nine steps. Arrived at the last one I beheld a vast expanse of water. To my right I heard the impetuous tumbling of torrents; to my left a cold rain mixed with masses of hail fell near me. I was contemplating this majestic scene when the star which had guided me to the platform and which was slowly swinging overhead, plunged into the gulf. Believing that I was reading the commands of the Most High, I threw myself into the midst of the waves. An invisible hand seized my lamp and placed it on the crown of my head. I breasted the foamy wave and struggled to reach the side opposite the one which I had left. At last I saw on the horizon a feeble gleam and hastened forward. Perspiration streamed down my face and I exhausted myself in vain efforts. The shore which I could scarcely discern seemed to recede to the degree I advanced. My strength was ebbing. I feared not to die, but to die without illumination . . . I lost courage, and lifting to the vault my tear-streaming eyes I cried out: "JUDICA JUDICIUM MEUM ET REDIME ME, PROPTER ELOQUIUM TUUM VIVIFICA ME." (Judge thou my judgment and redeem me, by thy eloquence make me live.) I could hardly move my tired limbs and was sinking more and more when near me I saw a boat. A richly dressed man guided it. I noticed that the prow was turned toward the shore which I had left. He drew near. A golden

XLIX

crown shone on his forehead. "VADE ME CUM," *said he,* "MECUM
PRINCIPIUM IN TERRIS, INSTRUAM TE IN VIA HAC QUA GRADUERIS."
(*Come with me, with me, the foremost in the world; I will
show thee the way thou must follow.*) *I instantly answered
him:* "BONUM EST SPERARE IN DOMINO QUAM CONSIDERE IN
PRINCIPIBUS." (*It is better to trust in the Lord than to sit
among the mighty.*) *Whereupon the boat sank and the mon-
arch with it. Fresh energy seemed to course through my veins
and I gained the goal of my efforts. I found myself on a shore
covered with green sand. A silver wall was before me inlaid
with two panels of red marble. Approaching I noticed on
one of them sacred script, the other being engraved with a
line of Greek letters; between the two plates was an iron circle.
Two lions, one red and the other black, rested on clouds and
appeared to guard a golden crown above them. Also near the
circle were to be seen a bow and two arrows. I read several
characters written on the flanks of one of the lions. I had
barely observed these different emblems when they vanished
together with the wall which contained them.*

SECTION FOUR

IN its place a lake of fire presented itself to my sight. Sulphur and bitumen rolled in flaming waves. I trembled. A loud voice commanded me to pass through the flames. I obeyed, and the flames seemed to have lost their power. For a long time I walked within the conflagration. Arrived at a circular space I contemplated the gorgeous spectacle which by the grace of heaven it was given me to enjoy.

Forty columns of fire ornamented the hall in which I found myself. One side of the columns shone with a white and vivid fire, the other side seemed to be in shadow; a blackish flame covered it. In the center of this place stood an altar in the form of a serpent. A greenish gold embellished its diapered scales in which the surrounding flames were reflected. Its eyes looked like rubies. A silvery inscription was placed near it and a rich sword had been driven into the ground near the serpent, on whose head rested a cup . . . I heard the choir of the celestial spirits and a voice said to me: "The end of thy labours draws near. Take the sword and smite the serpent."

I drew the sword from its sheath and approaching the altar I took the cup with one hand and with the other I struck a terrific blow upon the neck of the serpent. The sword rebounded and the blow re-echoed as if I had struck on a brass bell. No sooner had I obeyed the voice than the altar disappeared and the columns vanished in boundless space. The *sound which I had heard when striking the altar repeated itself as if a thousand blows had been struck at the same time. A hand seized me by the hair and lifted me toward the vault which opened to let me through. Shadowy phantoms appeared before me—Hydras, Lamias and serpents surrounded me. The sight of the sword in my hand scattered the foul throng even as the first rays of light dissipate the frail dream-children of the night. After mounting straight upward through the layers that composed the walls of the globe, I saw again the light of day.*

SECTION FIVE

SCARCELY had I risen to the surface of the earth, when my unseen guide led me still more swiftly. The velocity with which we sped through space can be compared with naught but itself. In an instant I had lost sight of the plains below. I noticed with astonishment that I had emerged from the bowels of the earth far from the country about Naples. A desert and some triangular masses were the only objects I could see. Soon, in spite of the trials which I had undergone, a new terror assailed me. The earth seemed to me only a vague cloud. I had been lifted to a tremendous height. My invisible guide left me and I descended again. For quite a long time I rolled through space; already the earth spread out before my confused vision . . . I could estimate how many minutes would pass until I would be crushed on the rocks. But quick as thought my guide darts down beside me, takes hold of me, lifts me up again, and again lets me fall. Finally he raises me with him to an immeasurable distance. I saw globes revolve around me and earths gravitate at my feet. Suddenly the genius who bore me touched my eyes and I swooned. I know not how long I remained in this condition. When I awoke I was lying on a luxurious cushion; the air I breathed was saturated with the fragrance of flowers . . . A blue robe spangled with golden stars had replaced my linen garment. A yellow altar stood opposite me from which a pure flame ascended having no other substance for its alimentation than the altar itself. Let-

ters in black were engraved at the base of the altar. A lighted torch stood beside it, shining like the sun; hovering above it was a bird with black feet, silvery body, a red head, black wings and a golden neck. It was in constant motion without however using its wings. It could only fly when in the midst of the flames. In its beak was a green branch; its name is

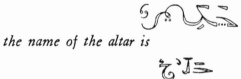

the name of the altar is

Altar, bird and torch are the symbol of all things. Nothing can be done without them. They themselves are all that is good and great. The name of the torch is

Four inscriptions surrounded these different emblems.

I TURNED aside and noticed an immense palace the base of which rested on clouds. Its mass was composed of marble and its form was triangular. Four tiers of columns were raised one above the other. A golden ball topped the edifice. The first tier of columns was white, the second black, the third green and the last one a brilliant red. I intended, after having admired this work of immortal artists, to return to the palace of the altar, the bird and the torch; I desired to study them further. They had disappeared and with my eyes I was searching for them when the doors of the palace opened. A venerable old man came forth clad in a robe like mine, except that a golden sun shone on his breast. His right hand held a green branch, the other upheld a censer. A wooden chain was about his neck and a pointed tiara like that of Zoroaster covered his white head. He came toward me, a benevolent smile on his lips. "Adore God" said he to me in Persian. "It is He who sustained thee in thy trials; His spirit was with thee. My son, thou hast let slip by the opportunity. Thou couldst have seized instantly the bird,

the torch

and the altar

Thou wouldst have become altar, bird and torch at one and

the same time. Now, in order to arrive at the most secret place of the Palace of sublime sciences, it will be necessary for thee to pass through all by-ways. Come . . . I must first of all present thee to my brothers." He took me by the hand and led me into a vast hall.

The eyes of the vulgar cannot conceive the form and richness of the ornaments which embellished it. Three hundred and sixty columns enclosed it on all sides. Suspended from a golden ring in the ceiling was a cross of red, white, blue and black. In the center of the hall was a triangular altar composed of the four elements; on its three points were placed the bird, the altar and the torch. "Their names are now changed," said my guide. Here the bird is called

אבפירדבא

the altar

כהנא

and the torch

בפירית

The hall is called

and the triangular altar

Around the altar were placed eighty-one thrones, to each of which one mounted by nine steps of unequal height, the treads being covered with red carpets.

While I was examining the thrones, a trumpet sounded whereupon the doors of the hall

swung on their hinges to let pass seventy-nine persons, all attired like my guide. Slowly they came near and seated themselves on the thrones while my guide stood beside me. An old man, distinguished from his brothers by a purple mantle the hem of which was covered with embroidered characters, arose, and my guide, addressing them in the sacred tongue, said: "Behold one of our children whom it is the will of God to make as great as his fathers." "May the will of the Lord be done," responded the old man, and turning to me he added: "My son, the time of thy physical trials is now ended ... There remain long journeys for thee to undertake. Henceforth thy name shall be

آللساٮ

Before thou visit this edifice, each of my eight brothers and myself will present thee with a gift." He walked up to me and with the kiss of peace gave me a cube of grey earth called

the second gave me three cylinders of black stone called

קבך

the third a small piece of rounded crystal called

كَزٮٳ

the fourth a crest of blue plumes named

اشتوٮشق

the fifth added a silver vase which carries the name of

בשם

the sixth gave me a cluster of grapes known by the sages under the name of

מזה רשא

the seventh presented me with the figure of a bird similar in its form to

הזהי

but it had not its brilliant hues; it was of silver. "It has the same name," he said to me; "it is for thee to give it the same virtues." The eighth gave me a small altar, resembling the altar

נפרית

Finally my guide placed in my hand a torch composed, like

פרה

of brilliant particles; however, it was not lighted. "It is for thee," he added, "like those that have preceded it to give it the same virtues." "Reflect on these gifts" then said the chief sage. "They all lead equally to perfection, but none of them is perfect in itself. It is from their admixture that the divine product must come. Know also that all of them are null if thou employ them not in the order in which thou hast received them. The second, which serves for the use of the first, remains merely crude matter without warmth and without usefulness unless in its turn it is aided by that which comes after it. Guard carefully the gifts thou hast received and set out upon thy journeys after thou hast drunk from the cup of life." Hereupon he handed me in a crystal cup a shining liquor of saffron hue; its taste was delicious and it emitted an exquisite aroma. I was about to hand the cup back to him after moistening my lips in the liquor, when the old man said: "Drink it all; it will be thy only nourishment during thy journeys." I obeyed and felt a divine fire course through all the fibers of my body. I was stronger, braver; even my intellectual powers seemed doubled.

I hastened to give the greeting of the wise men to the august assembly I was about to leave, and at my guide's command I entered a long gallery on my right hand.

SECTION SEVEN

A T the entrance of this gallery stood an oval steel
vessel which upon my approach filled with crystal-clear water, purified by fine white sand. The
vessel rested on three brass feet. A black panel
had engraved on it several characters on the side facing the
door. Near the vessel was a linen veil and above the vessel
two green marble columns supported a round marble placque.
One saw there, surrounded by two inscriptions, the figure of
the sacred seal formed of a cross in four colours, attached to
a golden crosspiece which upheld* two other concentric circles,
the larger one being black, the other red. To one of the
columns was attached a silver ax with a blue handle; it is called

קלקנתרם

After reading the inscriptions I went up to the vessel and
washed, first my hands, but finished by plunging in bodily.
I stayed there three days, and on coming out of the water I
saw that it had lost its transparency. Its sand had become
grayish and rust-coloured particles stirred in the fluid. I tried
to dry myself with the linen veil but fresh drops of water kept
taking the place of those the linen absorbed. I gave up trying
to dry myself with the veil and, keeping in the shade, I remained there motionless for six whole days. At the end of this
time the source of these waters was exhausted. I found that
I was dry and lighter though my strength seemed to be in-

* TWO CIRCLES WHICH SURROUND

LXI

creased. After walking about for a little while I returned to the vessel. The water which had been in it was gone. In its place was a reddish liquid; the sand was gray and metallic. I again bathed in it, being careful however to remain there only a few moments. When stepping out of it I noticed that I had absorbed part of the liquid. This time I did not try to dry myself with the cloth, for the liquor with which I was saturated was so strong and corrosive that it would have instantly destroyed the fabric. I found myself at the other end of the gallery stretched out on a bed of warm sand where I spent seven days. After this time I returned to the vessel. The water was as it had first appeared. Once more I plunged into it and after having washed myself carefully, came out. This time I had no difficulty in drying myself. Finally, after having purified myself according to the instructions I had received, I prepared to leave this gallery in which I had spent sixteen days.

SECTION EIGHT

I LEFT *the gallery by a low and narrow door and entered a circular apartment the panelling of which was made of ash and sandal wood. At the further end of the apartment on a pedestal composed of the trunk of a vine lay a mass of white and shining salt. Above was a picture showing a crowned white lion and a cluster of grapes; both rested on a salver sustained in the air by the smoke of a lighted brazier. To my right and left two doors opened, one giving unto an arid plain. A dry and scorching wind blew over it continually. The other door opened on a lake at the extreme end of which a black marble facade could be seen.*

I approached the altar and took into my hands some of the white and shining salt which the sages call

בּוֹּת רֵישָׁא

and rubbed my entire body with it. I impregnated myself with it, and after having read the hieroglyphics accompanying the picture I prepared to leave this hall. My first intention was to leave by the door opening upon the plain, but there issued therefrom a hot vapor and I preferred the opposite path. I had the freedom of choice with the condition, however, not to leave the one once chosen . . . I decided to cross the lake; its waters were sombre and sleeping. At a certain distance I clearly noticed a bridge called

اشتَان لَس

To reach it I would have been obliged to follow the windings

LXIII

of a shore covered with rocks, and I preferred to cross the lake. I entered the water which was as thick as cement. I noticed that it was useless for me to swim since my feet touched bottom everywhere. I walked in the lake for thirteen days. At last I came to the other shore.

SECTION NINE

THE earth was as dark as the water through which I had come. A hardly perceptible slope led me to the base of the building which I had seen from afar. On its long square front several characters were engraved like those used by the priests of ancient Persia. The entire building was made of rough black basalt; the doors, of cypress wood, opened to let me pass. A warm, moist wind arose suddenly and pushed me rapidly to the middle of the chamber at the same time closing the doors upon me . . . I was in darkness, but gradually my eyes grew accustomed to the meager light which reigned in this enclosure and I was able to discern the surrounding objects. The vaulting, the walls and the floor of the chamber were as black as ebony. Two mural paintings arrested my attention; one represented a horse such as our poets describe as having caused the downfall of Troy. From its gaping flanks a human corpse protruded. The other image showed a man long dead. Vile insects bred by putrefaction swarmed over his face and devoured the substance which had given them birth. One of the arms of the dead man, stripped of its flesh, already showed the bones. A man, dressed in red, standing by the corpse, endeavoured to lift it. A star shone on his forehead; his legs were enclosed in black buskins. Above, between and below the picture were three black panels bearing silver characters. I read them and then occupied the time by making the rounds of the hall where I was to spend nine days.

LXV

In a dark corner I found a pile of black earth which was fat and saturated with animal particles. I was about to take some of it when a thundering voice, like the sound of a trumpet, forbade me to do so, saying: "This earth has lain in this hall only eighty-seven years; when thirteen more years have elapsed, thou and the other children of God may use it." The voice fell silent, but its last ringing sounds continued to vibrate a long time in that temple of silence and death. After remaining in it the time prescribed, I departed by the door opposite to the one through which I had entered. I again saw the light, but it was not so strong around the black hall as to tire my eyes habituated to darkness.

I saw with surprise that in order to reach the other buildings I should have to cross a wider lake than the first one. For eighteen days I walked in the water. I recalled that when crossing the first lake its waters became darker and thicker as I advanced. The waters of this lake, on the contrary, became ever clearer the closer I approached the shore. My robe, which had in the palace become as black as the walls, seemed to me to be of a grayish hue; gradually it resumed its colours; however, it did not become entirely blue but was nearer to a beautiful green.

After eighteen days I ascended the embankment by means of a white marble platform. The name of the hall is

צֶחֹן

the first lake

צֶחֹן רֹאשׁ

the second

צֶחֹן אַחֲרִית

SECTION TEN

AT some distance from the shore a sumptuous palace raised aloft its alabaster columns; its different parts were joined by porticos of flame colour. The entire edifice was of light and airy architecture. As I approached the portals, I saw that the front was decorated with the figure of a butterfly. The doors stood open . . . I entered. The entire palace consisted of a single hall . . . surrounded by a triple colonnade, each rank composed of twenty-seven alabaster columns. In the middle of the building stood the figure of a man issuing from a tomb; his hand, holding up a lance, struck the stone which previously confined him. His loins were girt about with a green garment; gold gleamed from its hem. On his breast was a square tablet bearing several letters. Above this figure hung a golden crown and the figure seemed to lift itself into the air in order to seize the crown. Above it was a yellow stone tablet bearing several emblems which I explained by means of the inscription I saw on the tomb and by the one I had seen on the breast of the man.

I stayed in that hall which is called

بلسان ازدن

the time needful for contemplating all its aisles, and soon I left it with the intention of crossing a vast plain in order to reach a tower that I had perceived at quite some distance.

LXVII

SECTION ELEVEN

NO sooner had I quitted the steps of the palace when I saw fluttering in front of me a bird similar to

אספידכא

this one, however, having two wings like a butterfly's besides its own. A voice issuing from a cloud commanded me to seize and to affix it and I darted forth after it. It did not fly but used its wings in order to run with the greatest rapidity. I pursued it; it fled before me and made me cover the entire plain several times. I followed it without pause. Finally, after pursuing it for nine days, I forced it to enter the tower which I had seen in the distance as I was leaving

צחן

The walls of this edifice were of iron. Thirty-six columns of the same metal supported it. The interior was of the same material, incrusted with shining steel. The foundations of the tower were so constructed as to be twice as deep in the earth as they were high above ground. The bird had barely entered this enclosure when an icy cold seemed to overcome it. In vain it tried to move its numbed wings. It still fluttered, trying to flee, but so feebly that I reached it with the greatest ease.

I seized the bird, and driving a steel nail

בּרד נחשׁ שׁין

LXIX

*through its wings, I affixed it to the floor of the tower with
the aid of a hammer called*

ζ ſ ⊥ ᵥᵥᵢ

*Hardly had I finished when the bird acquired new strength.
It did not move, however, but its eyes began to shine like
topaz. I was gazing at it when my attention was attracted by
a group in the center of the hall. It showed a handsome man
in the prime of life. In his hand he held a staff about which
two serpents were interlaced. The young man was striving
to escape a larger and more powerful man who wore a girdle
and a helmet of iron surmounted by waving red plumes. Near
him a sword lay on a buckler covered with hieroglyphs. The
armed man held in his hand a heavy chain with which he
shackled the feet and body of the youth who tried in vain to
flee from his terrible adversary. Two red tablets bore certain
characters.*

*I departed from the tower, and opening a door between
two pillars I found myself in a vast hall.*

SECTION TWELVE

HE hall into which I had just entered was perfectly round; it resembled the interior of a globe composed of hard and transparent matter, as crystal, so that the light entered from all sides. Its lower part rested upon a vast basin filled with red sand. A gentle and equable warmth reigned in this circular enclosure. The sages call this hall

זלרף לֵּﬞ

The basin of sand sustaining it is called

אשא חרלית

With astonishment I gazed around this crystal globe when a new phenomenon excited my admiration. From the floor of the hall ascended a gentle vapor, moist and saffron yellow. It enveloped me, raised me gently and within thirty-six days bore me up to the upper part of the globe. Thereafter the vapor thinned; little by little I descended and finally found myself again on the floor. My robe had changed its colour. It had been green when I entered the hall, but now changed to a brilliant red. A contrary effect had taken place in the sand on which the globe rested. Gradually its red colour had been transformed into black. After finishing my ascent I remained three more days in that hall.

After that time I left it in order to enter a large place surrounded by colonnades and guilded porticos. In the center of

*the place stood a bronze pedestal supporting a group represent-
ing a large strong man whose majestic head was covered with
a crowned helmet. A blue garment protruded through the
meshes of his golden armour. In one hand he held a white
staff bearing certain characters, the other hand he extended
towards a beautiful woman. His companion wore no garment, but a sun radiated from her breast. Her right hand
held three globes joined by golden rings; a coronet of red
flowers confined her beautiful hair. She sprang into the air
and seemed to lift with her the warrior who accompanied her;
both were borne up by the clouds about the group. On the
capitals of four white marble columns were set four bronze
statues; they had wings and appeared to sound trumpets.*

*I crossed the place, and mounting on a marble platform
which was before me, I noticed with astonishment that I had
re-entered the hall of Thrones (the first in which I had found
myself when entering the Palace of Wisdom). The triangular
altar was still in the center of this hall but the bird, the altar
and the torch were joined and formed a single body. Near
them was a golden sun. The sword which I had brought
from the hall of fire lay a few paces distant on the cushion of
one of the thrones; I took up the sword and struck the sun,
reducing it to dust. I then touched it and each molecule became a golden sun like the one I had broken. At that instant
a loud and melodious voice exclaimed, "The work is perfect!"
Hearing this, the children of light hastened to join me, the
doors of immortality were opened to me, and the cloud which
covers the eyes of mortals, was dissipated. I SAW and the
spirits which preside over the elements knew me for their
master.*

FINIS

PHOTOSTATIC FACSIMILE OF
LA TRES SAINTE TRINOSOPHIE

[1]

Cest dans l'asile des criminels
dans les cachots de L'Inquisition, que
votre ami trace ces lignes qui doivent
servir à votre instruction. En songeant
aux avantages inapreciables que doit

[2]

sens d'adoucir les horreurs d'une captivité
aussi longue que peu méritée ... j'ai du
qplaisir a penser qu'environne de
gardes, chargé de fers, un esclave peut
encore élever son ami au dessus des —
puissants, des monarques qui gouvernent
ces lieu d'exil.

Vous allez pénétrer mon cher
Philochate dans le sanctuaire des —
sciences sublimes; ma main va lever
qpour vous le voile impénétrable qui
derobe aux yeux du vulguaire, le
tabernacle, le sanctuaire ou l'éternel
déposa les secrets de la nature secrets
qu'il reserve pour quelquisltres privilé-
-giés, pour les Elus que sa toute puis-

[3]

sance créas pour **VOIR** pour planer à
sa suite dans l'immensité de sa Gloire,
et détourner sur l'espèce humaine un
des Rayons qui brillent au tour de
son Throne d'or. —

    Puisse l'exemple de votre ami
être pour vous une leçon salutaire et
je bénirai les longues années d'épreuves
que les méchans m'ont fait subir. ....

    Deux écueils également
dangereux se présenteront sans cesse sur
vos pas l'un outragerois les droits sacrés
de chaque individu c'est L'Abus du
pouvoir que **DIEU** vous auroit confié,
l'autre causerois votre perte c'est
L'Indiscrétion .... tous deux sont nés

[4]

d'une même mere, tous deux doivens
l'existence a l'Orgueil, la foiblesse humaine les allaita, ils sons aveugles,
leur mere les conduis, par son secours
ces deux Monstres, vons porter leur
souffle impur jusque dans les cœurs
Des **Elus** du très haut malheur a
celui qui abuseroir Des dons du ciel
pour servir ses passions la main toute
puissante qui lui soumis les Ele-
mens, le briseroir comme un foible
Roseau une éternité De tourmens
pourrais a peine expier son crime
les Esprits Infernaux souriroiens
avec dedain aux pleurs De l'être
dons la voix menaçante les fit si

[5]

souvent trembler au sein de leurs
abimes de feu.

Ce n'est pas pour vous
Philochale que j'esquisse ce tableau
Effrayant, l'ami de l'humanité ne
deviendra jamais son persécuteur.....
mais l'Indiscretion, mon fils ce besoin
impérieux d'inspirer l'étonnement,
l'admiration, voila le précipice, que
je redoute pour vous. Dieu laisse
aux hommes le soin de punir le ministre
imprudent qui permet à l'œuil du
Prophâne de pénétrer dans le sanctuaire mystérieux, ô Philochale que mes
malheurs soient sans cesse présens
à votre esprit, & moi aussi j'ai connu

[6]

le bonheur, comblé des bienfaits du ciel
entouré d'une puissance telle que l'entendement humain ne peut la concevoir
commandant aux génies qui dirigent
le monde, heureux du bonheur que je
faisais naître, je goutais au sein
d'une famille adorée la félicité que
l'Éternel accorde à ses enfans chéris
un instant à tout détruit, j'ai parlé
et tout s'est évanoui comme un
nuage, ô mon fils ne suivez pas mes
traces .... qu'un vain désir de briller
aux yeux du monde ne cause pas
aussi votre perte .... pensez à moi,
c'est dans un cachot, le corps brisé
par les tortures que votre ami vous

écris; Philocale reflechisses que la main
qui trace ces caracteres porte l'empreinte
des fers qui l'acablent.... Dieu m'a
puni; mais quai-je fais aux hômes
cruels qui me persecutent? Quel
Droit ont-ils pour interoger le
ministre de l'Eternel? ils me des
- mandent quéles sont les preuves de
ma mission, mes témoins sont des
prodiges, mes deffenseurs mes vertus,
une vie intacte, un cœur pur, que
disje ai-je encore le droit de me
plaindre, jai parlé le tres haut
me livré sans force et sans puissan-
-ce aux fureurs des l'avare fanatisme,
le bras qui jadis pouvois renverser

[8]

une armée, peut à peine aujourd'hui
soulever les chaines qui l'appesantisse.

Je m'égare, je dois rendre grace
à l'éternelle Justice... le dieu ven-
-geur à pardonné à son enfant
repentant, un esprit Aërien a
franchi, les murs qui me séparent
du monde; resplendissant de lumi-
-ere, il s'est presenté devant moi
il a fixé le terme de ma captivité,
dans deux ans mes malheurs finiront.
mes bourreaux en entrant dans mon
cachot le trouveront desert et
bientot purifié par les 4 élémens
pur comme le génie du feu je
reprendrai le rang glorieux ou la

[9]

bonté Divine, ma élevé mais combien
ce terme est encore éloigné combien
deux années paroissent longues à
celui qui les passe dans les souffrances,
dans les humiliations, non contens de
me faire souffrir les suplices les plus
horribles mes persécuteurs ont employé
pour me tourmenter des moyens plus
surs plus odieux encore, ils ont appellé l'infamie sur ma tête, ils ont fait
de mon nom un objet d'opprobre,
les enfants des hommes reculent
avec effroi quand le hazard les a
fait approcher des murs de ma
prison, ils craignent qu'une vap-
-eur mortelle ne s'échappe par...

[10]

l'ouverture etroite qui laisse passer
comme a regret un rayon de lumi
ère dans mon cachot. Ô Philocale
c'est la le coup le plus cruel dont
ils pouvoient m'accabler . . . .

J'ignore encore si je pourrai
vous faire parvenir cet ouvrage . . .
Je juge des difficultés que j'éprouve
rai pour le faire sortir de ce lieu de
tourmens, par celles qu'il a fallu
vaincre pour le terminer, privé
de tout secours j'ai moi même com
posé les agens qui m'étaient néces
saires. Le feu de ma lampe quel
ques pièces de monnaies et peu de
substances chimiques échappées

[11]

aux regards scrutateurs de mes bourreaux
ont produit les couleurs qui ornent ce
fruit des loisirs d'un prisonnier . _
  Profitez des instructions de votre
malheureux ami, elles sont tellement
claires qu'il seroit a craindre que
ces écrit tombat en dautres mains _
que les votres... souvenez vous seu
_lement que tout doit vous servir _
une ligne mal expliquée un caractere
oublié, vous empêcheroient de lever le
voile que la main du créateur a _
posé sur le sphinx .
  Adieu Philocale ne me plai
_gnez pas la clemence de l'Éternel _
égale sa justice à la première . _

[12]

[14]

J'étois mais la lune cachée
par des nuages sombres ne jettois qu'une
lueur incertaine sur les blocs de lave
qui environnent la Solfatara. La tête
couverte du voile de Lin, tenant dans
mes mains le rameau d'or je m'avançois

sans crainte vers le lieu où j'avois reçu
l'ordre de passer la nuit. Errant
sur un sable brûlant, je le sentois
à chaque instant s'affaisser sous mes
pas les nuages s'ammoncelaient
sur ma tête; l'éclair sillonnait la
nue, et donnait une teinte sangl-
-ante aux flammes du volcan.....
Enfin j'arrive, je trouve un autel
de fer j'y place les rameau mystéri-
-eux..... Je prononce les mots redou-
-tables... a l'instant la terre tremble
sous mes pieds le tonnera éclate.....
les mugissements du Vésuve répon-
-dent à ces coups redoublés ses —
feux se joignent aux feux de la

[16]

foudre.... les cœurs des Genies s'éleverus dans les airs et se fons répéter aux échos les louanges du créateur... la branche consacrée. que j'avais placé sur l'autel triangulaire s'enflâme, tout à coup une épaisse fumée m'environne, je cesse de voir, plongé dans les ténèbres je crus descendre dans un abime, j'ignore... combien de temps je restai dans cette situation mais en ouvrant les yeux je cherchai vainement les objets qui m'entouraient quelquetems auparavant; l'autel de Vésuve la campagne de Naples avoient fui loin de mes yeux j'étois dans un vaste souterrain, seul, éloigné du monde entier... près de moi étoit une robe,

longue, blanche, son tissu délié me sembla
composé de fil de lin, sur une masse de
grains étais posé une lampe de cuivre
au dessus une table noire, chargée de
caractères grecs m'indiquaient la route
que je devois suivre je pris la lampe
et après avoir revêtu la robe je
m'engageai dans un chemin étroit
dont les parois étaient revêtus de marbre
noir. Il avait trois milles de longueur,
mes pas retentissaient d'une manière
effrayante sous ces voutes silencieuses
enfin je trouvai une porte elle condui-
sait à des degrés, je les descendis,
après avoir marché longtems je crus
appercevoir une lueur errante devant

[18]

moi je cachai ma lampe je fixai mes yeux
sur l'objet que j'entrevoyais il se dissipa
s'évanouit comme une ombre.

Sans reproches sur le passé sans —
crainte sur l'avenir je continuai ma
route elle devenait de plus en plus —
pénible .... toujours engagé dans des —
galeries composées des quartiers de pierres
noires ... je n'osais fixer le terme de —
mon voyage souterrain enfin après
une marche immense, j'arrivai à —
une place quarrée une porte s'ouvrait
au milieu de chacune de ses quatre —
faces elles étaient de couleur différen—
te es placées chacune à l'un des quatre
points cardinaux, j'entrai par celle

du septentrion elle étoit noire, celle qui
me faisoit face étoit rouge, la porte
de l'orient étoit bleue, celle qui lui
étoit opposée étoit d'une blancheur
éclatante ... au centre de cette salle
étoit une masse quarré, une étoile
de cristal brillait sur son milieu.
on voyoit une peinture sur la face
septentrionale elle représentait une
femme nue jusqu'à la ceinture, une
draperie noire lui tomboit sur les
genoux. deux bandes d'argent
ornaient son vêtement, dans sa
main étoit une baguette. elle la
pasoit sur le front d'un homme
placé vis-à-vis d'elle. une table terminée

[20]

par un seul pied étais entre eux deux
sur la table, étais une coupe et un
fer de lance. Une flame soudaine
s'élevait de terre et semblois se
diriger vers l'homme une inscription
expliquais le sujet de cette peinture.
Une autre m'indiquais les moyens
que je devois employer pour sortir
de cette salle.

Je voulus me retirer après
avoir considéré le tableau et l'étoile
j'allais entrer dans la porte rouge,
quand tournant sur ses gonds avec
un bruit épouvantable elle se referma devant moi, je voulois tenter
la même épreuve sur elle, au

[21]

décrois la couleur du ciel, elle ne se
forma point mais un bruit soudain
me fis détourner la tête, je vis
l'étoile sagitter, elle se détache roule
et se plonge rapidement dans
l'ouverture de la porte blanche, je
la suivis aussitôt.

[22]

arrivé à la derniere j'apperçus une
immense étendue d'eau; des torrens
impétueux se faisaient entendre
à ma droite, a gauche une pluie
froide mellée de masses de grêle
tombait pres de moi je consi-
derais cette scene majestueuse
quand l'étoile qui m'avait guidé
sur le perron et qui se balançait
lentement sur ma tête se plon-
gea dans le gouffre je crus lire
les ordres du très haut je me
precipitai au milieu des vagues
une main invisible saisit ma
lampe et la posa sur le somet
de ma tête. Je fendis l'onde

[25]

écumeuse et m'efforçai de gagner le
point opposé à celui dont j'étois
parti, enfin je vis à l'horison une
foible clarté, je me hatai, jetté au
milieu des eaux et la sueur couvroit
mon visage, je m'épuisais en vains
efforts la rive que je pouvois à peine
appercevoir sembloit fuir devant
moi à mesure que j'avançais, mes
forces m'abandonnaient, je ne
craignois pas de mourir, mais de
mourir sans être illuminé, je perdis
courage et levant vers la voute mes
yeux baignés de pleurs. Je m'écriai :
Judica judicium meum et redime
me, propter eloquium tuum vivifica me,

[26]

à peine pouvois-je agiter mes membres
fatigués j'enfonçais de plus en plus
quand j'apperçus près de moi une
barque, un homme couvert de riches
habits, la conduisoit, je remarquai
que la proue étoit tournée vers la
rive que j'avois quittée, il s'approcha,
une couronne d'or brilloit sur son
front vade me cum me dit-il, me
cum principium in terris, instruam
te in via hac quâ gradueris Je
lui répondis à l'instant bonum
est sperare in domino quam
considere in principibus ..... A
l'instant la barque, et le monar-
que s'abimerent dans le fleuve,

[27]

une force nouvelle sembla couler
dans mes veines je parvins a gagner
le bût de mes fatigues, je me trouvai
sur un rivage semé de sable vert.
Un mur d'argent étoit devant
moi deux lames de marbre rouge
étaient incrustées dans son épais
seur, j'approchai, l'une étoit chargé
de caractères sacrés sur l'autre
étoit gravée une ligne de lettres
grecques entre les deux lames
étoit un cercle de fer deux
lions, l'un rouge et l'autre noir,
reposaient sur des nuages et
semblaient garder une couronne
d'or placée au dessus deux, un

[28]

voyois encore près du cercle un arc
et deux flèches je lus quelques
caractères écrits sur les flancs d'un
des lions. à peine avais-je observé ces
differens emblêmes, qu'ils disparu-
rent avec la muraille qui les
contenait.

[30]

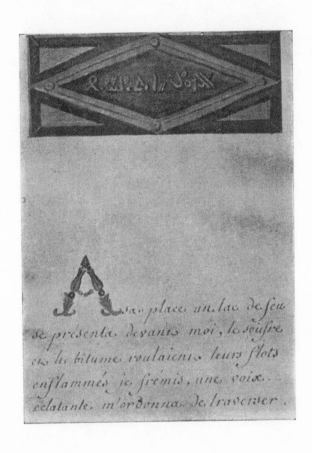

À sa place un lac de feu
se présenta devant moi, le soufre
et le bitume roulaient leurs flots
enflammés je frémis, une voix
éclatante m'ordonna de traverser.

ces flames. j'obeis et les flammes
semblerent avoir perdu leur acti-
-vité longtems je marchai au milieu
De l'incendie, arrivé dans un espace
circulaire, je contemplai le pompeux
spectacle dont la bonté du ciel
daignait me faire jouir.

Quarante colonnes de feu
décoraient la salle dans laquelle je
me trouvois un coté des colonnes bril-
-loit d'un feu blanc et vif, l'autre
sembloit dans l'ombre, une flame
noirâtre le couvrait; au centre de
ce lieu s'élevait un autel en forme
de serpent, un or vert embellissoit
son écaille diaprée sur la qu'elle se

[32]

reflettaient les flammes qui l'environ-
naient, ses yeux semblaient des
rubis, une inscription argentée étais
posée près de lui. Une riche épée étais
plantée en terre près du serpent,
une coupe reposoit sur sa tête....
J'entendis le cœur des esprits céles-
tes, une voix me dis le terme de tes
travaux approche, prends le glaive,
frappe le serpent.
Je tirai l'épée de son four
reau en m'approchant de l'autel.
je pris la coupe d'une main et de
l'autre je portai un coup terrible
sur le col du serpent. l'épée rebon-
dis, le coup raisonna comme si

javois frappé une cloche d'airain,
à peine avois-je obéi a la voix que
l'autel disparût les colonnes se per-
-dirent dans l'immensité, le son que
javois entendu en frappant l'autel
se répéta comme si mille coups
etaient frappés en même temps,
une main me saisit par les che-
-veux et m'éleva vers la voute, elle
souvrit pour me livrer passage,
des vains fantomes se présenterent
devant moi, des Hydres des Lamies
m'entourerent de serpens, la vue de
l'épée que je tenois a la main écarta
cette foule immonde comme les
premiers rayons du jour dissipent

[34]

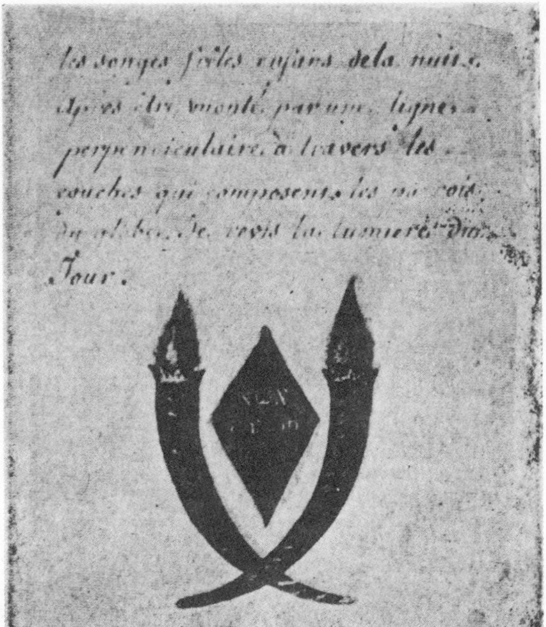

les songes frêles enfans dela nuit.
après être monté par une ligne
perpendiculaire à travers les
couches qui composent les [illegible]
du globe, je vois la lumiere du
Jour.

[36]

A peine, étais-je parvenu à la surface de la terre que mon conducteur invisible m'entraîna, plus rapidement encore, la vélocité avec laquelle nous parcourions les...

espaces aëriens ne peut être compa-
-rée à rien qu'a elle même ; en un
instant j'eus perdu de vue les plai-
-nes sur les qu'elles je dominais. —
j'avais observé avec étonnement que
j'étais sorti du sein de la terre, loin
des campagnes de Naples une —
plaine déserte. quelques masses tri-
-angulaires étaient les seuls objets —
que j'eusse apperçu. Bientôt mal-
-gré les épreuves que j'avois subies,
une nouvelle terreur vint m'assaillir,
la terre ne me semblait plus qu'un
nuage confus, j'étois élevé à une
hauteur immense, mon guide invi-
-sible m'abandonna. je redescendis-

[38]

pendant un assez long tems je
roulai dans l'espace ; déja la terre
se déployait a mes regards trou_
_blés ... je pouvois calculer combien
de minutes se passeraient avant
que j'aille me briser contre un
rocher. Bientôt, prompt côme
la pensée mon conducteur se
précipe apres moi il me reprend
m'enlève encore une fois, il me
laisse retomber, enfin il m'elève
avec lui `a une distance incom—
—mensurable, je voyois des globes
rouler autour de moi, des terres
graviter a mes pieds tous `a
coup le génie qui me portois

[39]

me touche les yeux, je perdis les
sentimens... J'ignore combien de
temps je passai en cet etat, à
mon réveil je me trouvai couché
sur un riche coussin; des fleurs
des aromates, embaumaient l'air
que je respirais.... Une robe
bleu semée d'étoiles d'or avoit
remplacé le vétement de lin.
vis-à-vis de moi étoit un autel.
Jaune, un feu pur s'en exallait
sans qu'aucune autre substance
que l'autel même l'alimentat.
Des caracteres noirs etaient
gravés sur sa baze. Auprès
étoit un flambeau allumé qui

brilloit comme le soleil.au.dessus
étoit un oiseau donts les pieds
étaient noirs, le corps d'argent;
la tête rouge les ailes noires es
Le Col d'or. Il s'agitait sans
cesse mais sans faire usage de
ses ailes. Il ne pouvoit voler
que lorsqu'il se trouvoit au milieu
des flammes. dans son bec étoit
une branche verte. son nom est
⟨symbole⟩ celui de l'autel
es ⟨symbole⟩ l'autel, l'oiseau es le
flambeau sous le symbole de tous,
rien ne peut être fait sans
eux, eux mêmes sous tous ce
qui est bon es grand. le flambeau

[41]

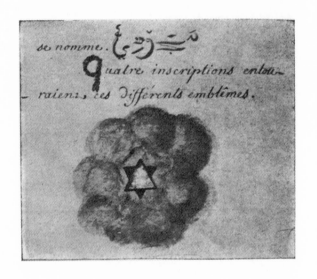

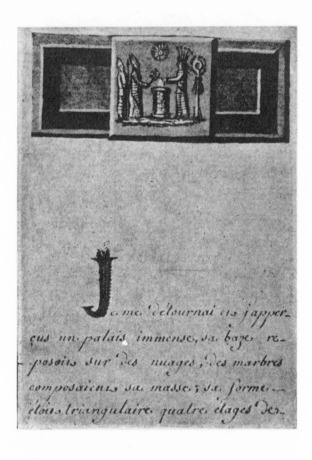

J c me detournai ci japper-
çus un palais immense, sa baze reposoit sur des nuages, des marbres
composaient sa masse; sa forme
étoit triangulaire, quatre étages des

colonnes s'élevaient les uns sur les autres.
Une boule dorée terminait cet édifice
le premier rang de colonne était blanc,
le second noir. le troisieme verd le der-
_nier était d'un rouge brillant, je
voulus apres avoir admiré cet ou-
_vrage des artistes eternels retourner au
lieu où étoient l'autel, l'Oiseau et
le flambeau, je voulois encore les
observer ils étoient disparus, je les
cherchois des yeux quand les portes
du palais s'ouvrirent, un vieillard
venerable en sortit, sa robe étoit
semblable à la mienne excepté
qu'un soleil doré brilloit sur sa
poitrine sa main droite tenoit

une branche verte, l'autre soutenois
un encensoir, une chaine de bois
eloie attachée à son col une thiare
pointue comme celle de zoroastre
couvroit sa tête blanchie, il s'approcha
de moi; le sourire de la bienveillance
erroit sur ses levres, "adore Dieu
me dit-il en langue Persane, c'est
lui qui t'a soutenu dans les épreuves
son esprit etoit avec toi, mon fils
tu as laissé fuir l'occasion tu pou-
vais à l'instant saisir l'oiseau
الله le flambeau ﷺ et
l'autel تاع أو لا سروي devenu
à la fois, autel oiseau, et flambeau... Il jouis à présent pour

[46]

parvenir au lieu le plus secret du
Palais des sciences sublimes que tu
en parcours tous les détours. viens..
Je dois avant tout te présenter à
mes freres. Il me prit la main et
m'introduisit dans une vaste salle.
Des yeux vulgaires ne peuvent
concevoir la forme et la richesse —
des ornemens qui l'embellissoient.
trois cent soixante colonnes l'entourai
-ent de toutes parts, au plafond étoit
une croix rouge, blanche, bleue et
noire. un anneau d'or la soutenoit
au centre de la salle étoit un autel
triangulaire, composé des quatre
élémens sur ses trois points étaient

posés l'oiseau, l'autel et le flambeau.
Ils ont changé de nom me dit mon
guide, ici on nomme l'oiseau אספירבא,
l'autel כהנא et le flambeau נמריר;
la salle est appellée . 𐤗𐤛 l'autel
triangulaire. ΑϴΑΝℿΡ autour de
l'autel étaient placés quatre-vingts
un Thrônes; on montait à chacun
par neuf marches de hauteur inégale;
des housses rouges les couvraient.

Pendant que j'examinois
les thrônes, le son d'une trompette
se fit entendre; à ce bruit les
portes de la salle 𐤗𐤛 tournèrent
sur leurs gonds pour laisser passer
soixante dix neuf personnes, toutes

[48]

vetues comme mon conducteur.
Elles s'approcherent lentement et
s'assirent sur les thrônes, mon guide
se tint de bout auprès de moi. Un
viellard distingué de ses frères par
un manteau de pourpre dont les
bords etaient chargée de caractères
en broderies, se leva et mon guide
prenant la parole en langue sacré
Voila dit-il un de nos enfans que
Dieu veut rendre aussi grand que
ses peres. Que la volonté du seigne-
-ur s'accomplisse répondit le viellard.
Mon fils ajouta til en s'adressant à
moi votre temps d'epreuves physiques
est accompli.... Il vous reste à faire

de grand voyage, désormais vous vous appellerez ٱلْكَعْبَة avant de parcourir cet édifice, huit de mes frères et moi allons vous faire, chacun un présent il vint a moi et me dóña avec le baiser de paix, un cube de terre grise on le nomme خَجَر le second trois cylindres de pierre noire appelé קבב le troisième, un morceau de cristal arrondi, on l'appele בולא le quatrième, une aigrette de plumes bleues nommée قشة le cinquième, y joignis un vase d'argent, qui porte le nom de בשם le sixième, une grappe de raisin connue parmi les Juifs sous le nom de עין מצ le septième,

[50]

me presenta, une figure, d'oiseau sembla_
_ble, pour la forme, a הזהי mais il
n'avoit pas ses brillantes couleurs; il
etoit d'argent, il porte le même nom
me dit il, c'est à toi a lui donner les _
mêmes vertus. le huitième me donna
un petit autel ressemblant, aussi à l'au_
_tel נפרית enfin mon conducteur me
mis dans main un flambeau compo
sé comme אברה de particules brillan
tes mais il etoit eteint. c'est à toi ajou
_tatil comme ceux qui l'avoient précédé
à lui donner les mêmes vertus, réfléchis_
sur ceci dous, me dit ensuite le chef _
des sages tous tendent egalement à
la perfection, mais nul n'est parfait

par lui même, c'est de leur mélange —
que doit sortir l'ouvrage divin. sache
encore que tous sont nuls si tu ne les
emploie suivant l'ordre dans le qu'el
ils t'ont été donné. le second qui sera
a employer le premier ne seroit qu'
— une matiere brute sans chaleur, sans
utilité sans le secours de celui qui vient
après lui, garde soigneusement les
présens que tu as reçu et comence
tes voyages après avoir bû dans la
coupe de vie. Il me presenta dans
une coupe de cristal une liqueur
brillante et safrancée son gout étoit
délicieux un parfum exquis s'en exal
— loit. Je voulus rendre la coupe après

[52]

avoir trempé mes levres dans la liqueur,
achève, me dit le vieillard, ce breuvage
sera la seule nouriture que tu prendras
pendant le temps de tes voyages. J'obéis
et je sentis un feu divin parcourir
tous les fibres de mon corps, j'étois plus
forts, plus courageux, mes facultés même,
intellectuelles, semblaient être doublées.

Je me hatai de donner le salut des
sages à l'auguste assemblée que j'allais
quitter, et par les ordres de mon conducteur, je m'enfonçai dans une longue
galerie qui se trouvois à ma droite.

[54]

A l'entrée de la galerie dans
la qu'elle je me trouvois étoit posée une
cuve d'acier, a mon approche elle se
remplits d'une eau pure comme le cris-
-tal, qui vints s'epurer sur un sable.

blanc et fin.la cuve étois ovale ; Elle
étois soutenue sur trois pieds d'airain.
une lame noire incrustée sur le coté
qui regardois la porte renfermois
quelques caractères. près dela cuve
étois un voile de lin. au dessus d'elle
deux colonnes de marbre vert. suppor
-tois une plaque de marbre arrondie.
On y voyois entouré de deux inscrip-
-tions la figure du cachet sacré.
formée d'une croix de quatre couleurs,
attachée à une traverse d'or qui sou-
-tient deux autres cercles concentriques
-le plus grand noir. l'autre rouge. à
l'une des colonnes étois attachée une
hache d'argent dont la hampe étois

deux cercles quintouroius

bleue elle s'appelle קקקותם après avoir
lû les inscriptions, je m'approchai de la
cuve et je m'y lavai, en commençant
par les mains, je finis par m'y plon-
-ger, tout entier. J'y restai trois jours,
en sortant de l'eau je m'apperçus
qu'elle avoit perdu sa transparence,
son sable étoit devenu grisâtre, des
particules couleur de rouille s'agittai-
-ent dans le fluide. Je voulus me
secher avec le secours du voile de lin,
mais de nouvelles gouttes d'eau rem-
-plaçaient sans cesse celles dont le
linge s'imbibait je renonçai à me
secher avec le voile et me tenant à
l'ombre j'y restai immobile pendant

[57]

six jours entiers; au bout de ce temps la
source de ces eaux fut tarie je me
trouvai sec et plus leger quoique mes
forces me parussent augmentées, après
m'être promené quelque temps je re-
tournai a la Cuve, l'eau quelle con-
-tenoit étoit epuisée, a sa place étoit
une liqueur rougeâtre, le sable étoit
gris et metallique. Je m'y baignai de
nouveau, en observant cependant de
n'y rester que quelques instans, en me
retirant je vis que j'avois absorbé une
partie du liquide, cette fois je ne cher-
-tai pas de tarir avec le linge, la liqu-
-eur dont j'étois imprégné, elle l'au-
-roies detruit a l'instant, toutes elles

[58]

étois forte. et corrosive . Je fus à l'autre
bout de la gallerie m'étendre sur un
lit de sable chaud, j'y passai sept jours
au bout de ce temps je revins à la
cuve l'eau étoit semblable a la premi-
-ere., je m'y replongeai et en ressortis
apres m'être lavé avec soin. cette fois
je parvins sans peine à m'essuyer,
enfin apres m'être purifié selon
les instructions que j'avois reçu, je
me disposai à sortir de cette gale-
-rie. apres y être resté seize jours.

[60]

Je quittai la galerie par une
porte basse et étroite et j'entrai
dans un appartement circulaire
ses lambris étaient de bois de frê-
ne et de santal au fond de l'ap-

[61]

partement sur un socle composé
de seps de vigne reposait une
masse de sel blanc et brillant,
au dessus étoit un tableau il représentoit un lion blanc couronné, et
une grappe de raisin, ils étoient
posés sur un même plateau, que
la fumée d'un brasier allumé
élevoit dans les airs. et ma droite
et à ma gauche souvraient deux
portes l'une donnoit sur une
plaine aride. Un vent sec et
brulant y régnoit en tous temps.
l'autre porte souvroit sur un lac
à l'extrémité du quel on apper-
cevoit une façade de marbre noir.

Je m'approchai près de l'autel et pris dans mes mains du sel blanc et brillant que les sages appellent מלח ישר je m'en frottai tout le corps... Je m'en pénétrai et après avoir lu les hieroglyphes qui accompagnoient le tableau je m'apprêtai à quitter cette salle. mon premier dessein etoit de sortir par la porte qui donnoit sur la plaine, mais une vapeur brûlante s'en exalloit, je préférai le chemin opposé. j'avois la liberté de choisir, avec la condition cependant de ne pas quitter celui que j'aurois pris... Je me décidai à passer le lac, ses eaux

[63]

eaux sombres et dormantes, j'apper-
-cevois bien à une certaine distance un
pont nommé ... Wilhelms je préférai
traverser le lac à la longue route que
j'aurois été obligé de faire pour attein-
-dre le pont, en suivant les sinuosités
d'un rivage semé de rochers. je entrai
dans l'eau, elle étoit épaisse comme
... je m'apperçus qu'il...
m'étoit inutile de nager, par tout
mes pieds rencontrèrent le sol. Je
marchai dans le lac pendant treize
jours. Enfin je parvins à l'autre ...

La terre etoit d'une couleur foncée comme l'eau dans la qu'elle j'avois voyagé, une pente insensi-ble me conduisit au pied de l'edifi-ce que j'avois apperçu de loin, sa

forme étoit un quarré long, sur le fron-
-ton étoient gravés quelques caracte-
-res, semblables à ceux qu'employ-
-aient les Prêtres des anciens Per-
-sans. l'édifice entier étoit bâti de
Basalte, noir dépoli: les portes étoient
de bois de ciprès. Elles s'ouvrirent
pour me laisser passer; un vent
chaud et humide s'élevant tout
à coup me poussa rapidement
jusqu'au milieu de la salle et en
même temps referma les portes sur
moi... Je me trouvai dans l'obscu-
-rité, peu à peu mes yeux s'accou-
-tumerent au peu de lumière qui
régnoit dans cette enceinte, et je

[67]

pûs distinguer les objets qui m'entou-
-raient. la voute, les parois, le plan-
-cher de la salle étoient noirs comme
l'ébène, deux tableaux peints sur la
muraille fixerent mon attention,
l'un representoit un cheval tel
que les poëtes nous peignent celui
qui causa la ruine de Troie! De
ses flancs entrouverts sortoit un
cadavre humain. L'autre peinture
offroit l'image d'un homme mort,
depuis longtems, les vils insectes
enfans dela putrefaction, s'agit-
-taient sur son visage et déva-
-raient la substance qui les avoit
fais naitre, un des bras décharnés

de la figure morte, laissoit déja ap-
-percevoir les os ; placé près du cadavre,
un homme vetu de rouge s'efforçoit
de le relever, une étoille brilloit
sur son front, des brodequins noirs
couvroient ses jambes, trois lames
noires chargées de caracteres d'argent
etoient posées au dessus, entre et
au dessous des tableaux. Je les lus,
et m'occupai à parcourir la salle
ou je devois passer neuf jours . .

   Dans un coin plus obscur
se trouvoit un monçeau de terre noire,
grasse et saturée de particules ani-
-males, je voulus en prendre, une
voix éclatante comme le son d'une

trompette me le défendia, il n'y a que
quatre vingts sept ans que cette terre est
posée dans cette salle me dis-elle
quand treize autres années seront
écoulées, toi et les autres enfans de
Dieu pourront en user. La voix se
tut mais les derniers sons vibrèrent
long temps dans ce temple du silence
et de la mort. Après y être resté le
temps prescrit je sortis par la porte
opposée à celle par la qu'elle j'étois
entré. Je revis la lumière, mais elle
n'étoit pas assez vive autour de la
salle noire, pour fatiguer mes yeux
habitués à l'obscurité.
Je vis avec étonnement qu'il

[70]

me falloit pour joindre les autres édifi-
-ces traverser un lac plus large que le
premier, je marchai dans l'eau pen-
-dant dix huit jours. Je me souvins-
que dans la première traversée les-
eaux du lac devenoient plus noires-
et plus épaisses à mesure que j'avan-
-çois, au contraire dans celle ici-
plus j'approchais de la rive, et plus
les eaux s'éclaircissoient. Ma robe,
qui dans le palais étoit devenue-
noire comme les murailles me parut-
alors d'une teinte grisâtre, elle reprit
peu à peu ses couleurs, cependant-
elle n'étoit pas entièrement bleue,
mais approchant d'un beau vert-

[71]

Après dix huit jours je mon-
-tai sur le rivage par un perron de
marbre blanc; la salle est nomée.
צחן le premier lac צון ראש
le second צחן אחריה

[73]

A quel que distance du
rivage un palais somptueux elevoit
dans les airs ses colonnes d'albâtre,
ses differentes parties étoient jointes
par des portiques couleur de feu, tous

l'édifice étoit d'une architecture légère
et aérienne. Je m'approchai des portes,
sur le fronton étoit représenté un
papillon. Les portes étoient ouvertes...
J'entrai, le palais entier ne formoit
qu'une seule salle... trois rangs de
colonnes l'entouroient, chaque rang
étoit composé de vingt-sept colonnes d'albâtre. Au centre de l'édifice
étoit une figure d'homme, elle sortoit
d'un tombeau sa main appuyée
sur une lance frappoit la pierre
qui la renfermoit autrefois, une draperie verte, ceignoit ses reins l'or
brilloit au bas de son vêtement
sur sa poitrine étoit une table

[75]

quarrée, sur laqu'elle je distinguai
quelques lettres. Au dessus de la figure,
étois suspendue une couronne d'or,
elle sembloit s'élever dans les airs
pour la saisir. Au dessus de la
couronne étoit une table de pierre
jaune, sur laqu'elle étoient gravés
quelques emblêmes, je les expliquai
par le secours de l'inscription que j'ap-
-perçus sur le tombeau, et par celle
que j'avois vûe sur la poitrine de
l'homme. Je restai dans cette salle
appellée ... le temps nécessaire
pour en contempler tous les détours.
et j'en sortis bientôt dans l'intention

[76]

de me rendre a travers une vaste
plaine a une tour que j'apperçus
a une assez grande distance.

[78]

À peine j'avois quitté les marches du palais, que j'apperçus voltiger devant moi un oiseau semblable à אספירבא mais celui ci avoit deux ailes de papillon outre les siennes.

une voix sortant d'un nuage m'ordoña
de le saisir et de l'attacher. Je m'élan_
_çai après lui, il ne voloit pas mais il
se servoit de ses ailes pour courir avec
la plus grande rapidité, je le poursuivis,
il fuyoit devant moi et me fit plusieurs
fois parcourir la plaine dans toute son
étendue, je le suivis sans m'arreter. —
enfin après neuf jours de course, je
le contraignis d'entrer dans la tour
que j'avois vù de loin en sortant de
א־X les murailles de cet
édifice étoit de fer. trente six pilliers
de même métal les soutenoit. l'inté_
rieur étoit de même matière, incrus
_té d'acier brillant. Les fondemens ..

[80]

de la tour étoient construits de telle
manière, que sa hauteur étoit doublée
sous terre. à peine l'oiseau fut il en-
-tré dans cette enceinte, qu'un froid
glacial sembla s'emparer de lui il fit
de vains efforts pour mouvoir ses ailes
engourdies. Il s'agitloit encore, essay-
-ant de fuir, mais si foiblement que
je l'atteignis avec la plus grande facilité.

Je le saisis, et lui passant
un clou d'acier à travers les ailes je
l'attachai sur le plancher de la tour.
à l'aide d'un marteau, appellé ז ל וה
à peine avois-je fini que l'oiseau re-
-pris de nouvelles forces, il ne s'agitta
plus, mais ses yeux devinrent ‒‒

מרח נווה ✝

brillants comme des topazes j'étois
occupé à l'examiner quand un grou-
-pe placé au centre de la salle
attira mon attention, il représentoit
un bel homme dans la fleur de
l'age, il tenoit à la main une verge
qu'entouraient deux serpens entre-
-lacés, et s'efforçait de s'échapper
des mains d'un autre homme grand
et vigoureux, armé d'une ceinture
et d'un casque de fer sur lequel
flottoit une aigrette rouge; une épée
étoit près de lui elle étoit appuyée
sur un bouclier chargé d'hieroglyphes;
l'homme armé tenoit dans ses mains
une forte chaine il en lioit les pieds

[82]

et le corps de l'adolescent qui cherchoit
vainement à fuir son terrible ad-
-versaire; deux tables rouges renfer-
-maient des caracteres.

Je quittai, la tour et ouvrant
une porte qui se trouvoit entre
deux pillers je me trouvai dans
une vaste salle.

[84]

La salle dans la qu'elle je
venois d'entrer étois éxactement ron-
de, elle ressembloit à l'intérieur d'une
boule, composée d'une matiere dure
et diaphane comme le cristal —
elle recevoit du jour par toutes ses.

parties. La partie inférieure étoit ..
posée sur un vaste bassin rempli
de sable rouge, une chaleur douce
et égale regnoit dans cette enceinte circulaire. Les sages nomment
cette salle. מלכות le bassin de sable
qui la soutient porte le nom de
יסוד je considerois avec étonement
ce globe de cristal quand un phéno-
mène nouveau exita mon admiration. Du plancher de la salle s'éleva
une vapeur douce, moite et safra-
née elle m'environna, me souleva
doucement et dans l'espace de
trente six jours me porta jusqu'à
la partie supérieure du globe, après

[86]

ce temps la vapeur s'affaiblir, je
descendis peu à peu enfin je me
retrouvai sur le plancher. ma robe
changea de couleur, elle étoit verte
lorsque j'entrai dans la salle, elle
devint alors d'une couleur rouge
éclatante. Par un effet contraire
le sable sur lequel reposait le
globe, quitta sa couleur rouge et
devint noir par degrés je demeu-
-rai encore trois jours dans la
salle. après la fin de mon ascension.
Après ce temps j'en sortis
pour entrer dans une vaste place
environnée de colonnades et de por-
-tiques voris au milieu de la place étoit

un pied d'estal de bronze, il supportoit
un grouppe qui présentoit l'image
d'un homme grand et fort, sa tête
majestueuse étoit couverte d'un cas-
-que couronné; a travers les mailles
de son armure d'or, sortoit un
vêtement bleu; il tenoit d'une
main un bâton blanc, chargé de
caracteres, et tendoit l'autre a une
belle femme; aucun vêtement ne
couvroit sa compagne, un soleil
brilloit sur son sein, sa main
droite supportoit trois globes joints
par des anneaux d'or, une couroñe
de fleurs rouges ceignoit ses beaux
cheveux, elle s'élançoit dans les

[88]

airs en sembloin, y élever avec elle le
guerrier qui l'accompagnoir.; tous..
les deux. etoiens portés sur des nuages
autour du groupe., sur les chapiteaux.
De quatre colonnes de marbre. blanc,
etoient posés quatre statues 'de bron_
ze ; elles avoient Des ailes en parois
_saient, sonner de la trompette.
    Je traversai la place., en mon_
_tant un perron 'de marbre. qui se
trouvoit devant moi, je vis avec
étonnement que je rentrois dans la
salle des thrônes, (la première où je
m'étois trouvé en arrivant au pa_
lais De la sagesse) l'autel triangu
_laire étoit toujours au centre de celle.

salle mais l'oiseau, l'autel et le flambeau
étoient réunis et ne formoient plus
qu'un corps. Très deux étois pasé
un soleil d'or, l'épée que j'avois ap_
_porté de la salle de feu, reposoit à
quel que pas de là sur le coussin d'un
des thrônes; je pris l'épée et frapant
le soleil je le réduisis en poussière,
je le touchai ensuite et chaque mo_
lécule devint un soleil d'or sembla
_ble à celui que j'avois brisé. l'œuvre
est parfait s'écria à l'instant une
voix forte et mélodieuse, à ce cri
les enfans de la lumière s'empresse_
_rent de venir me joindre, les portes
de l'immortalité me furent ouvertes,

le nuage qui couvre les yeux des mor-
-tels, se dissipa. Je Vis et les esprits,
qui présidents aux élémens, me re-
-connurents pour leur maitre.

FIN

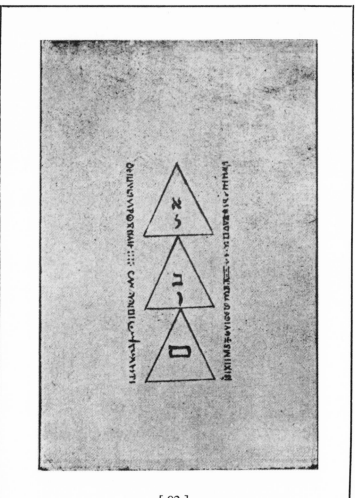

[93]

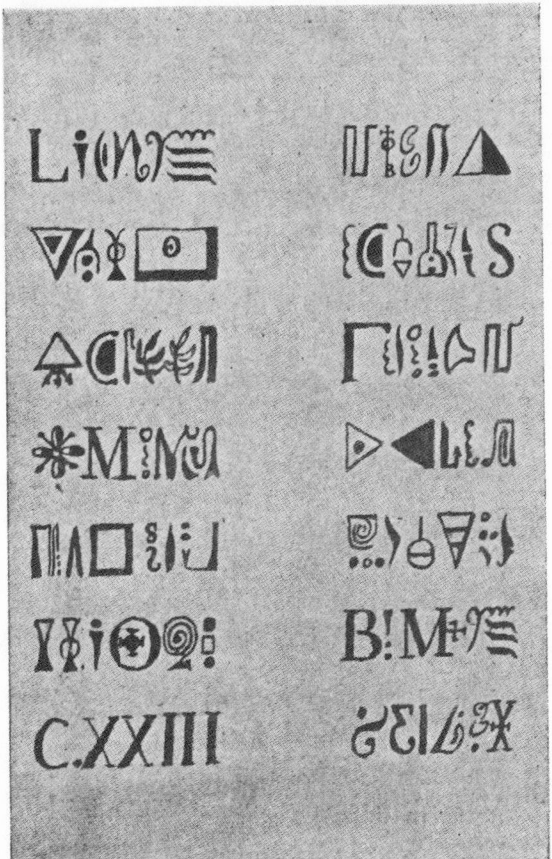

[96]

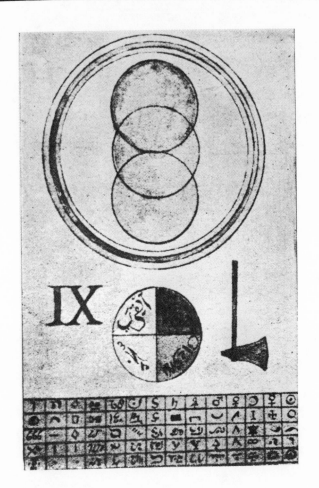

[97]

NOTES AND COMMENTARIES

INITIATION into the Mysteries was defined by the ancient philosophers as life's supreme adventure and as the greatest good that can be conferred upon the human soul during its terrestrial sojourn. Plato, in the Phaedrus, writes thus of the supreme importance of acceptance into the sacred Rites: "Likewise, in consequence of this divine initiation, we become spectators of entire, simple, immovable and blessed visions in a pure light; and were, ourselves, pure and immaculate and *liberated from this surrounding vestment which we denominated body,* and to which we are now bound as an oyster to its shell."

St. Paul also refers to the "inner experience" by which we come to KNOW. He says, "We speak of wisdom among the perfect, not the wisdom of this world, nor of the Archons (Rulers) of this world, but divine wisdom in a mystery, secret, which none of the Archons of this world know." An initiation is an extension of consciousness toward an appreciation of universal realities. The mystical ceremonials of the pagans and early Christians were but the outward symbols of inward processes. By obscure rites and pageantries the precious arcana of perfection was transmitted from age to age. The profane were satisfied by the solemnity of the outward forms and rituals, but the Adepts, those who had received the keys, applied the wisdom which was locked within the allegories to perfecting their internal spiritual faculties. Origen, the most mystical of the anti-Nicean fathers, in his preface to St. John, admits the twofold nature of all theological revelations: "To the literal minded (or exoterici) we teach the Gospel in the historic way, preaching Jesus Christ and Him crucified; but to the proficient, fired with the love of Divine Wisdom (the esoterici) we impart the Logos (the Word).

Perfection is not bestowed: it is achieved. Men do not become wise merely through the witnessing of sacred dramas . . . rather, by the understanding of them. Symbolism is the language of divine truths, a writing by means of which may be intimated things which it is unlawful to actually reveal. "For the mystic symbols are well known to us who belong to the Brotherhood." (Plutarch). By initiation the rule of works is established. The divine man and the divine in man are brought to completeness by works alone. The adepts of the old schools were "wise Master Builders" with vision to see, with courage to do, and wisdom to remain silent. "There is a secrecy and silence observed in all Mysteries," wrote Tertullian, the creator of ecclesiastic Latinity.

During the ceremonials of initiation the neophyte was given the LAW. The great verities by which the universe moves towards its inevitable identity with God were revealed. It remained for the Initiate to apply this Law and through this application to achieve conscious immortality. There is a forking of the ways of knowledge at which practice diverges from theory. A man may either fulfill the Law and thus by enlightened action come finally to perfection, or he may accept the word of the Law and, ignoring the spirit of it, remain as he is . . . imperfect and unenlightened. He who receives the LOGOS and abides in the spirit thereof gradually increases in wisdom. The Nazarean theurgists said of such a one that "he had an oath." He was dedicated to the release of his inner part from the domination of his outer senses and appetites. Says Aretaeus, "Until the soul is set free it works within the body and is obscured by vapors and clay." By vapors is arcanely signified the appetites and excesses of the emotions which are as substanceless as a mist, and by the clay is meant the unresponsiveness of the corporeal form.

To increase in wisdom is to increase in enlightenment, for by enlightenment is inferred the illumining of the inner recesses of the reason by the light of the Logos—the spiritual sun. This development of the ability to know by philosophic discipline is accompanied by extensions of realization and appreciation. These extensions are the true growth of the soul which increases towards inclusiveness. Hence, in the sacred writings, this expansion of the soul's sphere of action is called initiation. By initiation the indwelling divinity verges towards its own cause, the eternal Good. The chambers of initiation are the "many mansions" through which the indwelling divinity must pass as through the tortuous windings of the Cretan labyrinth. Along its course are many doors, through each of which it is ushered into a larger and more luminous area of function and action. With each increase of our ability to appreciate the magnitudes of the divine plan, we are said to be reborn. Rebirth is the passing out from an old condition into a new state, from an old limitation to a new extension. As we grow in knowledge, our universe seems to enlarge with us, taking on the measure of our new constitution. Wisdom releases.

The academies of the old Mysteries invited the wisest and best of humanity to depart from the mortal shadow of worldliness and devote itself to those labors which are truly eternal.

The perfection of Self is the Great Work, the beginning and end of wisdom: the perfected Self is the perfect offering and the consummation of the Great Work. He who is perfect is of the greatest use to others, the greatest good to himself and the most acceptable offering to the Most High.

With the collapse of the old pagan world and the corruption of the early Christian Church, the Mysteries ceased as great institutions. Their doctrines were lost, their priestcrafts were scattered, and their temples fell to ruin. New theories, for the most part superficial and insufficient, took the place of the earlier wisdom; and education, divorced from its spiritual part, laid the foundation for our present chaos. But the wise remained true to the ancient Rites. Those who had received the arcana could not, did not, forget. They gathered in secret, taught in secret and worshipped in secret. The temple fire burned in the hearts of its initiates. The outer forms crumbled away; but the inner spirit, strengthened by its participation in an everlasting truth, was immortal. Out of the darkness of a degenerate civilization, across the desert of sterile centuries, and finally through the Red Sea of the Inquisition the Mystics of the ancient wisdom carried triumphantly the Ark of their covenant.

The so-called Middle Ages were an era of fantastic symbolism. The Hermetists devised composite monsters borrowed from the gods of Egypt; the Cabbalists illuminated vellum with curious figures, seals, pentacles, and grotesque signatures of demons; the alchemists filled huge volumes with weird formulas telling of the mystic properties of toads and dragon's blood. In the dark field of medieval superstition there also grew and blossomed the Mystic Rose, to be finally choked out by the weeds of bigotry. These were strange centuries when false faith had put wisdom to hazard. Yet who dares to deny that the mystical traditions endured, and, clothed in the terms of Egyptian myths and chemistry, were still available to such as had eyes to perceive the tortured truth?

Against the background of dogmatic ignorance and purposeless pedantry stands out sharply and clearly the luminous personality of the Comte de St.-Germain. Master of the old wisdom, wise in forgotten truths, proficient in all the curious arts of antiquity, learned beyond any other man of the modern world, the mysterious Comte personified in his own incredible achievements the metaphysical traditions of fifty centuries. A thousand times the questions have been asked: where did St.-Germain secure his astonishing knowledge of natural law? How did he perpetuate himself from century to century, defying the natural corruption which brings prince, priest, and pauper alike to a common end? St.-Germain was the mouthpiece and representative of the brotherhood of philosophers which had descended in an unbroken line from the hierophants of Greece and Egypt. He had received the Logos. By his wisdom he confounded the elders. The life of this one man puts to naught the scholastic smugness of two thousand years.

La Très Sainte Trinosophie is supremely significant in that it sets forth the spiritual processes which finally result in adeptship. It is the diary of the soul's coming of age. It may well be the actual record of St.-Germain's own acceptance into the mystical brotherhood of which he finally became the Grand Master. As the purpose of the manuscript was the instruction of disciples already familiar with the secret terminology, the whole account is set forth symbolically in fragments of ritual and allegory derived from the ceremonials of the classical era. Though the first reading may serve only to perplex, a deep and careful analysis of the text will gradually enlighten. Each will discover in the writing that which he himself knows, he will interpret it according to that which he himself is, and he will apply it according to that which he himself desires. Symbols are all things to all men, yet beneath the wide diversity of interpretations of which they are susceptible is a wisdom simple and inevitable which can be comprehended only by the truly wise. Opinions, theories, and beliefs fall away; at the root of every emblem is a fact. Our manuscript is rich in these veiled facts and we are reminded by the author that no part of it is without hidden significance.

La Très Sainte Trinosophie is divided into twelve sections. Each is illuminated by an appropriate design. The early sections seem to derive their inspiration from the neo-Egyptian ritual called the Rite of Memphis, and the trials of the candidate are concerned directly with the four elements—earth, water, fire, and air. The grand pattern for the whole document is the Zodiac, to the signs of which the twelve sections of the writing are related. The Zodiac is the great soul cycle and the sun's passage through the zodiacal symbols is the original from which the ancient priestcrafts derived the authority for their sacred circumambulations. The ancients accepted the first sign of the zodiac as the beginning and the last sign as the end of all mundane activity. Similarly, Aries typified the beginning of regeneration or the entrance of the soul into light at the vernal equinox of the philosophic cycle, while Pisces signified the completion of the sacred pilgrimage and the accomplishment of the Magnum Opus.

St.-Germain chiefly employs alchemical symbols in this book of The Threefold Wisdom. This in no way infers that he is actually writing of chemical processes, for, as most of the great alchemists have agreed, the manufacturing of material gold is the least part of their science. That St.-Germain's meaning may be clear and the correlations between the zodiacal signs and the alchemical processes become evident, the following table will prove useful:

Aries	Calcination	Expulsion of the animal soul through heat. (Purification by the fire of aspiration.)
Taurus	Congelation	The union of parts; the achievement of one-pointedness or purpose.
Gemini	Fixation	The condition of becoming firm, the fixing of the will.
Cancer	Dissolution	To dissolve or to suspend in a fluid state; the universalizing of the personality.
Leo	Digestion	To soften by heat and moisture; to perfect the mind in wisdom (heat) and imagination (humidity).
Virgo	Distillation	The separation of the volatile principle from substance; the release of the soul from its involvement in bodily limitation.
Libra	Sublimation	The refining of elemental bodies; the increasing of the vibratory harmonies of the body.

Scorpio	Separation or Putrefaction	The philosophic death; an artificial decay by which the spiritual and material elements are separated from each other.
Sagittarius	Incineration	The burning away of dross; the soul fire consumes the external body.
Capricorn	Fermentation	The conversion of organic substance into new compounds by a ferment; the building of the Golden Man.
Aquarius	Multiplication	The process of increasing; adeptship.
Pisces	Projection	The process of transmuting base substance into Gold; the perfection of the Work; immortality; in the eastern tradition, Buddhahood.

The arrangement of these symbols and processes differs in minor degree among the various writers, but the principle is always the same—the transmutation of the not-Self into the Self; the tincturing of the outer life with the inner grace; the projection of soul upon its physical environment; the sublimation of evil into good; the multiplication of beauty, love, and truth until finally the powder of projection (wisdom) shall tincture the whole world. The alchemists tell us that a minute particle of the "Red Lion" can transmute into the purest gold a hundred thousand times its own weight. Wisdom—

and wisdom alone—can accomplish this, for one wise man can perfect the ages, and a little truth will in time so greatly increase that the universe may not contain it.

A ritual not dissimilar to that contained in the present writing is set forth in the Popol Vuh, the sacred book of the Quiche Indians of Central America. The neophyte, in his quest for wisdom, passes in succession through twelve tests: He crosses a river of blood (Aries) then a river of mud (Taurus), he detects a subterfuge (Gemini), he enters the house of darkness (Cancer), then the house of spears (Leo), the house of cold (Virgo), the house of tigers (Libra), the house of fire (Scorpio), and the house of bats (Sagittarius) where he dies (incineration). The picture at the head of the ninth section of St.-Germain's book depicts death. The body of the Indian neophyte is burned on a scaffold (Capricorn), the ashes scattered on the river (Aquarius), the ashes turn into a man-fish (Pisces), in which form the initiate, who has completed the cycle, destroys the evil genius who was his adversary through the initiatory ritual. The twelve Princes of Xibalba who are the Keepers of the Mysteries are of course the zodiacal gods.

As we follow St.-Germain into the lava beds of Vesuvius we indeed "tread upon the threshold of Persephone." We follow him in his soul quest for truth. Now we read only the symbols and we understand only in part, but ultimately we must achieve as he achieved and face the universal course with the same high courage that pressed him on to mastership. His symbols are from the Book of Life, and although we do not see in daily incident and happening the tests of which he writes, still each in his own sphere of experience faces the same hazards herein defined. We wander in the caverns of uncertainty; the ghostly forms of doubt harass us; fear steals away our strength, selfishness our vision, and ignorance our courage. But we are all alchemists in the laboratory of life: each is distilling the elixir of experience. In due time each shall have accomplished the perfection of this mysterious alchemical fluid, and with it shall tincture his world and himself. Upon the base metals of this present age he shall sprinkle the magical powder which his soul has discovered; the ages of Iron, of Silver, of Copper, and of Lead shall vanish away, and the Golden Age of the philosophers shall shine forth.

INTERPRETATION OF FIGURES AND TEXT

SECTION I.

(*Figure I,* page 1)   The highly decorated title page of the manuscript is a valuable key to the interpretation of the entire work. De Givry describes the emblems thus: "This author's symbolism is Egyptianized in the fashion of the day. On the title page of the work * * * we find * * * the bird of Hermes, a tree with golden fruit, and a vase in which the work is achieved, the primitive material under the form of a ball embraced by two wings, and a luminous triangle containing the Divine Name." In another place he adds: "The Hebrew name *El* is on the right with another divine name lower down written in Arabic; the letters *AB* near the latter are indicative of the alphabet and represent the Word—The Divine Word. On the left is a Hebrew inscription taken from the first verses of the Book of Genesis: 'And the earth was without form, and void (Tohu-vah-Bohu); and darkness was upon the face of the deep. And the Spirit of God (Ruach Elohim) moved upon the face of the waters.' "

The letters in the golden triangle do not form the sacred name *Jehovah* but, when decoded, yield the cryptic words: "Breathe after this One." That the "soul breath" of the Cabbalists is to be inferred is evident from the wings behind the hawk of Ra in the upper left corner. The second square from the top at the right is of especial Freemasonic interest. A candidate for initiation into the Mysteries stands in symbolic posture before an altar—with "one shoe off and one shoe on." The Hebrew letters *AL* (*EL*) in the small circle are one of the ten Cabbalistic names of God signifying "God, the Creator," and is associated with the Sephira Chesed or mercy. The letters AB are the mystical signature of the writer who was a "father" (abba) or master of the secret wisdom. The letters are also an abbreviation for an alchemical process. The Arabic "divine name" really consists of Hebrew words written in Arabic characters which read: "The Lord, the Most High, purifies." The Hebrew inscription in the lower left corner, while unquestionably the second verse of the first chapter of Genesis, does not read as in the Authorized Version. Characters have been changed and the sense altered to read in substance: "And the earth shall be a desolate waste. There shall be lamenting, and hate and consternation shall be upon the Face. And the Breath of El-him, because of the presence of the spirit, shall destroy those that have departed from God."

Analysis of the Text.

In the opening chapter of his manuscript, St.-Germain ingeniously depicts the "relapsed" state of the human soul. The dungeon of the Inquisition is the sphere of man's animal consciousness. The physical world, dominated by inquisitional impulses, constitutes the soul's torture chamber and house of testing. To the sage the material universe is the antechamber where gather those who are awaiting acceptance into the sacred rites. When the Comte speaks of "this place of exile" and the "monarchs who rule" over it, he refers to the illusionary universe and "the princes of this world." Here is the Prometheus myth, the Titan bound to Caucasus for indiscretion, and Lucifer chained in the bottomless pit for pride.

Throughout the early pages is traceable the allegory of the Prodigal Son. First is depicted humanity's heroic state during the Golden Age before sin and death came into the world. St.-Germain describes himself as "showered with the blessings of heaven and surrounded by power such as the human mind cannot conceive." The Comte then writes that "one moment destroyed everything." The mystery of the Fall of Man has never been revealed to the profane. The great cyclic law which swept the hosts of fiery Sparks into the abyss is known only to the elect. In the darkness of chaos the rebel spirits established their world. They built the cosmos and were locked within each of the material elements which they had willed into being. When the lower earth had been completed, the great Father desired to draw back into Himself His prodigal creation. To accomplish this He caused to issue from His own being His WORD—the Soter or Messiah. Descending from the Abode of Light this heavenly Archon diminished its splendor, and investing its glory in the dark robes of earth, took upon Itself the cross of the cycles.

To the Gnostics, the physical universe was compounded of the dregs of spirit. It was the abortion of space. Material existence was nature's punishment for the rebellion of the angels. This was clearly set forth in the initiatory rituals which taught that men were reborn in earthly bodies as punishment for sin. Those who perfected themselves were born no more, but, like Buddha at the Great Release, passed on to the Nirvana of the wise—a birthless, deathless state. From the dungeons of materiality the sages released themselves through the practice of their esoteric rites. Perfected in wisdom, these Initiates broke through the adamantine wall of the mortal sphere and emerged into the light of God.

The alchemical interpretation relates to the elementary spirits locked within the physical forms of the elements. It should be noted that in his procedure through the initiatory trials, St.-Germain identifies *himself* with the substance from which the Philosopher's Stone is to be formed. He is the alchemical *matter* itself passing through twelve cycles of refinement. It thus becomes evident that the alchemists recognized that their Great Work consisted of the transmutation of themselves. The earth (the dungeon) is filled with the seed souls of precious metals; here they are locked awaiting Art and Wisdom. As gold exists within every grain of sand but is incapable of manifesting itself unless stimulated by alchemical processes, so the seeds of truth, beauty, and knowledge exist within the dark earth of man's animal organism. The growth and perfection of these precious virtues is stimulated by discipline and in the fullness of time all base impulses and purposes are transmuted into the gold of soul power.

SECTION II

(*Figure II*, page 14)   In his notes on the *Trinosophia*, de Givry concerns himself solely with the alchemical import of the symbolism of this figure. He says of the second plate that it "represents a man gazing into a prophetic cup forming a magic mirror. The conjoined signs of the Sun and the Moon are seen against the pedestal of the table; at the top of the figure a super-position of differently colored rectangles indicates the phases of the Work; and the double sign of the lingam in a circle emblematically recalls the Hermetic male and female. An inscription in Greek letters and made-up characters gives a formula for the composition of Gold, or the Sun-King, by means of a mixture of gold and silver regenerated by vital mercury; linked to the blue rectangle giving this formula is a lower red rectangle inscribed with the rule for the furnace fire in Hebrew characters."

A careful analysis inclines us to suspect a more profound significance. The circle at the upper right, though possibly phallic in its superficial sense, is actually an occult monogram or seal containing two Greek letters. Translated these signify "the Light of God" or "the Light of Revelation." The rectangles at the upper left are the elements. The arrangement is Oriental. The lower four are crowned by the fifth—the quintessence, the mysterious Ether of the sages. The inscription in the upper panel describes the quickening of the soul seed by the warmth of the eastern quarter. (Aries.) There is also reference to the Breath which moves in the vessel, or upon the waters. The number 62 appears, accompanied by the admonition to open the heavenly gate (clairvoyance) with the aid of the vessel or cup. Does the cup (ark) contain the Water of Lethe, by partaking of which souls descending into generation lose all memory of their heavenly origin? Or does it contain the Water of Mnemosyne which flows at the gateway of wisdom and of which the adepts drink, the water of remembrance by which the soul remembers its own substance and origin?

The female figure is Isis in her role of Initiatrix. She is Nature, and her black skirt is the corporeal world by which part of her body is concealed. The naked man is the neophyte. Unclothed he came into the world and unclothed he must be born again. Bereft of all adornment, stripped of rank and power, he may bring to the temple nothing that he has—only that which he is.

The table upheld by the Sun and Moon and at the base of which burns the everlasting fire, is the world. The objects lying upon it, or held by Isis, are three of the suit symbols which appear upon Tarot cards. The whole design, in fact, is not dissimilar to that major Tarot trump which is called Le Bateleur, the Juggler. The *cup* is the symbol of water, the *spearhead* of fire and the *wand* of air. Fire, air, and water are the symbols of the great Magical Agent. Their names in Hebrew are Chamah, Ruach, and Majim, and by the Cabbala the first letter of each of these words—*Ch, R,* and *M*—constitute Chiram, known to Freemasons as Hiram. This is the invisible essence which is the father of the four elements, and designates itself Chiram Telat Mechasot—Chiram the Universal Agent, one in essence, three in aspect, in which is hidden the wisdom of the whole world.

The Hebrew characters in the panel above the head of Isis are translated: "On account of distress they shall cling to the Bestower," which means that those (the wise) who have become wearied with worldiness shall turn to wisdom, the bestower of all good things.

Analysis of the Text.

The account of the initiatory ritual now begins. The disciple has waited the appointed time in the dark material universe which is the womb of the Mysteries. The process of philosophical birth proceeds according to the ancient and immutable law. The neophyte, veiled and bearing the Golden Bough (the mistletoe), advances toward the iron altar.

The choice of Vesuvius as the scene for the initiation is exceedingly appropriate. The vent of the volcano leads downward into the subterranean strata of the earth where dwell the subterranean deities who must be first propitiated. The volcano is also the symbol of the alchemical furnace. The veil signifies that the neophyte has reached the state of the mystæ —one who perceives through a veil, or, in the Christian Mysteries, "as through a glass darkly." Pliny refers to the mistletoe as the "all-healer." It was presumably the Golden Bough given to Æneas as a passport to the infernal regions. Sir James Frazer thus comments upon the initiatory ceremony as set forth by Virgil:

"If the mistletoe, as a yellow withered bough in the sad autumn woods, was conceived to contain the seed of fire, what better companion could a forlorn wanderer in the nether shades take with him than a bough that would be a lamp to his feet as well as a rod and staff to his hands? Armed with it he might boldly confront the dreadful spectres that would cross his path on his adventurous journey. Hence when Æneas, emerging from the forest, comes to the banks of Styx, winding slow with sluggish stream through the infernal marsh, and the surly ferryman refuses him passage in his boat, he has but to draw the Golden Bough from his bosom and hold it up, and straightway the blusterer quails at the sight and meekly receives the hero into his crazy bark, which sinks deep in the water under the unusual weight of the living man."

Mistletoe is a parasite, and as such symbolizes the heavenly man within the mortal body. The soul grows from the body and in it, but is not of it, for as the tree takes its nourishment from the earth even so the body receives its sustenance from material sources; but the mistletoe derives its vitality not from the dark loam but from the tree and the air. The mistletoe is said to be luminous in the darkness, and has been called the wise man's torch. Its luminosity is the light of the internal organs—the aura of the brain. He who bears the branch announces his fitness to receive the initiation.

The neophyte lays the branch upon the iron altar; he gives himself to the law, assuming the responsibilities of spiritual progress. The sacred Word is spoken. The hallowed Bough

bursts into flame: the sacrifice is accepted. The earth opens.
Down through the Royal Arches as into a great abyss passes
the candidate.   The mists clear, revealing a vast cavern—the
dark mother from which all things must come—similar in
significance to Porphyry's cave of the nymphs. The long white
robe is the seamless garment of the Nazarene woven from the
endless thread of experience. The copper lamp is enlightened
love, without which no man may follow the narrow path of
wisdom.   Robed in purity, illumined with compassion and
understanding, the neophyte follows the black vaulted passage
which leads to immortality.

After a great distance the passage ends in a square room
from which lead four doors. This is the Hall of Choosing.
The doors signify the courses which the soul can pursue. The
black door is the path of asceticism and labor; the red door
is that of faith; the blue door is that of purification, and the
white door is that of adeptship and of the highest Mysteries.
In the Bhagavad-Gita, Krishna describes these paths and those
who follow them, and reveals that the last is the highest and
the most perfect.

The neophyte enters through the black door of asceticism
and labor and is about to pass through the red door of enlightened love when it closes upon him. He then turns to the
door of purification and sacrifice but this will not receive him.
Then the star, the symbol of his essential dæmon or genius,
darts through the white door. Fate has decreed adeptship.
The neophyte follows his star.

The alchemical significance of the account reveals that at
the beginning of the Great Work the power of choice is given
to the operator, that he may decide the end to which his labor
shall be directed. The black door represents the making of
material gold; the red door the Universal Medicine for the

healing of the nations; the blue door the Elixir of Life, and the white door the Philosopher's Stone. From the door which is chosen we discover that aspect of the Great Work which our author contemplates.

SECTION III.

(*Figure III,* page 23)   Two lions, one red and the other black, guard the Crown. The Crown is Kether, the fountain of wisdom. The king of beasts symbolizes nobility and rulership. In ancient times, figures of lions adorned the thrones of princes. These animals were also guardians of gates, and in Egypt the Sphinx, the man-headed lioness guarded the entrance to the House of the Mysteries.

The inscription upon the flank of the lion is inverted. An inverted symbol signifies a perverted power: thus, nobility becomes tyranny and greatness leads to despotism. In the introduction to his writing, St.-Germain warns his disciples of two adversaries which the neophyte must overcome. One he terms the *misuse of power* and the other *indiscretion.* The black lion represents tyranny and the red lion, lust. Those who would accomplish wisdom must overcome these animals if they would reach the Crown which lies beyond. The black lion is the temptation of power—the impulse to build temporal empire in a spiritual universe. The red lion is the temptation to possess. Its ministers in the human body are the sense perceptions which deflect the aspiring candidate from his holy course and lead him into the fantastic sphere of appetite and desire. There can be no compromise with these monsters of perversion.

With the vision there appears suspended the strung bow of the will and two lance-pointed arrows. Quickly must the bow be drawn and to the heart of each beast a shaft be driven.

"Kill out desire," decrees the eastern master. "Slay ambition," wrote the western sage. The clouds upon which the lions stand signify the unsubstantiality of the world's pomp and circumstance, while in the clear sky above, the Golden Crown floats unsupported. Wisdom is a sufficient foundation for itself, but all other bodies and conditions depend for their support upon the frail stuff "that dreams are made on."

The panel above the lions commands that man should bend the knee and worship the all-powerful God who sends forth His love in winged splendor from the first angle of the world. (Aries.) It also informs that the sixth sign, which is mighty and powerful, is the ending and completion of the ages. Virgo, the sixth sign of the zodiac, is the symbol of service and renunciation by which the lions may be overcome. He who gives up life for wisdom shall receive a fuller life.

Beneath the lions is a panel containing Greek characters which mean: "Each must sprinkle himself with his own wine from the mountain of Chios. He must drink to God before the wood. He must give himself in exchange for that for which he yearns." These words are from an old ritual. Wood was the symbol of Dionysius and it was in honor of this god of the wood and of the vine that the ritual of the Communion was first established. To drink of one's own blood or to sprinkle oneself with his own wine is to be immersed in or tinctured by the inner soul power. Fermentation was the presence of Bacchus or the life in the juice of the grape, and the Greeks used the symbol of intoxication, as do the Sufis of Islam, to represent ecstacy. A man in an ecstatic state was described by them as being one "intoxicated with God."

Analysis of the Text.

The first initiation is that of *earth,* represented by the black passage-ways in the subterranean regions of the volcano. To pass this test the body must be subdued in all its parts and become a perfect instrument of the enlightened will. The bodily atoms and molecules must be vibrated anew until there is no part of the physical fabric which does not pulsate with spiritually directed energy.

The second mystery in the order of the Memphis Rite is that of *water,* and at the beginning of this section the candidate finds himself standing on the shore of a vast underground lake. This is the sea of ether which separates the two worlds. It is the humidic body of the earth, the sphere of generation. He who would reach the invisible world must cross this sea, that is, become master of the generative powers of nature. Led by the blazing star, the candidate throws himself into the midst of the waves. With his lamp upon the crown of his head (the spirit fire lifted into the pineal gland) he struggles for mastery over the currents of the etheric world. His strength fails, and he cries out to the Universal Cause for help. A boat appears, in it seated the king of the earth with a golden crown upon his forehead. But the boat is pointed *back* toward the shore from which the neophyte has come. The crowned man offers the kingdoms of the earth but the disciple of wisdom who has risen above these things cannot be thus easily tempted. Strengthened by the courage of righteous decision and aided by the invisible genii, the candidate fights his way to the distant shore. Before him rises the silvery wall of the moon, the lady of the sea, whose dominion he has passed.

The *fire* initiation awaits him. Having mastered the vital principle of nature by which growth and propagation are controlled, the candidate next faces ambition, the fire of pride and the flaming tyranny of emotional excess. He beholds the lions, the fire symbols. The key to the course of action is revealed by the hieroglyphics. The lions, the writing and the wall dissolve. The path stretches out through the sphere of eternal flame.

The alchemical aspect of the symbolism is one of purification or the passing of the elements of the Stone through a bath. In this process of purification they pass from an earthy state through a vaporous or watery condition, to a fiery or gaseous quality. The lunar humidity present in all bodies must be dried out, which led the Greek philosophers to declare that "a dry soul is a wise one." The Platonists interpreted this to mean that the mastery of the lunar principle brought to an end the reign of corruption by which all bodies are finally dissolved. The moon rules physical generation or the perpetuation of corruptible forms, but the sun has dominion over spiritual generation, the creation of incorruptible bodies. Man is the progeny of fire (the sun), water (the moon), and air (the bird of Thoth). The temptation by the king with the golden crown suggests one of the most common difficulties of the alchemical tradition. Those who attempted the art in most cases failed in their quest for wisdom because they became fascinated with dreams of wealth. Material gold tempts the alchemist away from his spiritual quest for enlightenment and immortality.

SECTION IV.

(*Figure IV*, page 30)   Upon an altar formed of the twelve whorls of a winged serpent twisted about a spear rests the cup of Everlastingness. The device is derived from the cyclic serpent so often used in the Rites of Serapis. The twelve coils of the snake are emblematic of the philosophic year and the spiral course of the sun through the zodiacal constellations. In the preparation of the Wise Man's Stone the elements pass through twelve stages of augmentation. In each of these cycles the power of the *matter* is intensified, a fact which is suggested by the increasing size of the serpent's spirals. The figure is also reminiscent of what the sages termed the philosophic vortex— the natural form of the soul power in the human body.

In *Isis Unveiled,* H. P. Blavatsky writes: "Before our globe had become eggshaped or round it was a long trail of cosmic dust or fire-mist, moving and writhing like a serpent. This, say the explanations, was the Spirit of God moving on the Chaos until its breath had incubated cosmic matter and made it assume the annular shape * * *." In the *Chaldean Oracles* the Universal Fire is described as moving with a serpentine motion. The present symbol is the Universal Wisdom moving as a winged serpent upon the surface of the primitive chaos— that is, the unregenerated body of the neophyte. The ritual of the Sabazian Mysteries included the drawing of a live snake across the breast of the candidate. In the drawing, the serpent is twisted around the backbone—the spear—and forms an appropriate support for the cup of immortality.

Beside this strange altar stands the jewelled sword. Faintly traceable upon its sheath are the ancient symbols of the eye, the heart, and the mouth, symbolic of the three persons of the Creative Triad—life in the heart, light in the eye, breath in the mouth. The life, the light, and the breath are the sources of all things and from their union in the cruciform symbol the candidate must fashion the weapon for his protection against the elemental darkness. The cycle symbol must be overcome by wisdom. This is "the sword of quick decision" with which the Oriental neophyte must cut low the snaky branches of the world banyan tree, the emblem of the self-replenishing cycles and the law of rebirth. The serpent is the spiral of evolution; the cup contains the shining Nirvanic sea into which the soul is finally merged; the sword is the *illumined will*—the same sword which solves the enigma of life's Gordian Knot by cutting it with a single stroke.

The cryptic words on the upper panel carry out this thought. Translated, they are: "Reverence this vessel (the ark or cup) of Everlastingness; offer freely of yourself a portion unto *IA* (Iah or Jah, Jehovah) and to the corner (or angle) in atonement." This is derived from the symbolism of the Chaldeans, who regarded the Universal Cause as the Lord of the Angles.

Analysis of the Text.

The candidate enters upon the place of fire. A great sea of flames (the astral world) stretches out in every direction, bubbling and seething with an infernal fury. The dæmon orders the candidate to advance. With his mind fixed upon Reality, the disciple obeys, only to discover that the fire has lost its heat, and he walks unharmed into the midst of the conflagration. He finds himself in the Temple of Sidereal Fire, in the midst of which is the greenish-gold form of a serpent with ruby eyes and diapered scales. The nature of the fire is clearly revealed, for we are told that one-half of it burns with a vivid light, while the other half is shadowed and blackish. Here is the serpent of the astral light, which, according to Eliphas Levi, is twined around every flower that grows in the garden of Kama, or desire. The yogi in his meditation knows well the meaning of the House of Fire and the serpent which guards it. Here the candidate discovers the significance of the Universal Fire-Spirit which, turned downward, is the root of all evil, but if it be lifted up, draws all men to wisdom. The serpent-fire must be overcome. The sword is at hand, and with it the candidate strikes at the brazen coils. Brass is the composite metal symbolic of the body of man, before it is reduced by philosophy to its simple elements.

The Lord of the Fire World is vanquished. The senses are controlled; the appetites are under the iron dominion of the will. Anger, hate, and pride have been exiled from the soul. The three fires of illusion have died out. The whole mirage of the astral light fades amidst a terrifying outburst of sound and color. The candidate is lifted through the Arches of the underworld. He passes quickly through the monsters that dwell on the boundaries of excess. The cruciform sword scatters the foul throng of darkness. Upward and upward, through the numerous layers of the globe (the orbits of the interior stars) the neophyte rises, after his three days (degrees) in the darkness of Hades. The stone is rolled away, and at last, with a burst of glory, he rises into the light of day—the *air* sphere where dwells the mind which must be conquered next.

The alchemical philosophy is evident. The circular space is a distilling vessel which stands in the midst of the furnace flame. The serpent represents elements within the retort, and the candidate portrays other elements which have the power to dissolve and corrode the serpent. The rising of the candidate upward through the walls of the globe here signifies the vapors which, ascending through the long neck of the distilling vessel, escape from the heated inferno below.

SECTION V.

(*Figure V, page 36*) The strange bird hovering above the altar fire is the sacred Ibis, symbol of Thoth, the Egyptian god of wisdom and letters, and the patron of alchemy. It is the volatile philosophical Mercury which can remain in a suspended state only "when in the midst of the flames." By the philosophical Mercury we must understand the regenerated principle of intellect—mind rendered truly luminous by the flame of inspiration. In its beak the bird carries a green branch, the acacia of Freemasonry—the symbol of rebirth and immortality through spiritual enlightenment. The black feet and wings signify the *earth* principle, the silvery body the *water* principle, the red head the *fire* principle, and the golden neck the *airy* principle. The spiritual bodies of the elements are thus united in a philosophical creature, the bird of the wise men—the phœnix.

Beside the *bird* and the *altar* is an elaborate candlestick, its base formed of twisted serpents. (Ida and Pingala?) The upper end of the candlestick terminates in a lotus blossom from which rises a lighted taper. This is the soul light, the inner radiance which reveals the secret of the bird. As man's external existence is lighted by an external sun, by which he perceives all temporal concerns, so his internal existence is illuminated by the light of the soul, the radiance of which renders visible the workings of the divine mind within.

The inscription beneath reads: "To the strong is given the burden." This refers to the qualification for adeptship. The great truths of life can be conferred only upon those who have been tested in the essentials of character and understanding. In the panel above, the reader is instructed to "Kindle a fire upon the high place, that the sacrifice may be borne upward to the Desired One." The symbolism is borrowed from the ceremonials of the old Jews. Upon the altar of burnt incense a fire was continually burning. This is the fire of holy aspiration which consumes the base elements of the body and transmutes them into soul qualities, symbolized by the incense fumes, and these ascend as evidence of the spiritual convenant between aspiring humanity and its Creator.

The panel to the right describes the ceremony which accompanies the building of the sacred fire. The one on the left is part of a ritual, in substance as follows: "When the years of this existence are done, and the soul, outbreathing at death, approaches the gate of immortality, may the bird bear it swiftly away to the abode of the wise." In the Egyptian rites, the soul of the Initiate departed in the form of a bird which is shown hovering over the couch on which the mummy lies. The soul-bird with the green branch refers to the Messianic Mystery as set forth in the *Book of the Dead*. Wisdom confers immortality upon the soul. Without wisdom, the soul must perish with the body. This is the secret of the ritual of the *Coming Forth by Day or the Breathing Out of the Ka.*

Analysis of the Text.

The candidate next experienced the mystery of the *airy* or intellectual principle. He is raised out of the subterranean depths by his guardian spirit and lifted into the higher atmosphere. Below him is the desert. Special attention is called to triangular masses—the pyramids. An early manuscript in our collection affirms that the Egyptians were able to manufacture the Philosopher's Stone without artificial heat by burying the retort in the desert sand, which furnished the exact temperature for alchemical experiments. The desert is here a symbol for the aridity and unproductivity of the unawakened consciousness. In the physical universe spiritual values languish, yet in the midst of this mortal sphere stand the pyramids, supreme symbols of spiritual alchemy—temples of initiation in the desert of waiting. It is significant that the atmosphere of Egypt is peculiarly conducive to the perpetuation of ancient monuments of learning which, when moved from their old footings, rapidly crumble away. Thus material life, the desert, is a natural laboratory in which the supreme chemistry is accomplished through suffering and aspiration.

The account of the rising and falling of the candidate

through space relates to the alternations of the substances in the retort by which they pass through a cycle of attenuation and precipitation, to be finally drawn off through the neck of the vessel. Hermes uses this figure to set forth the mystery of rebirth, the periodic alternation of the soul from a temporal to a sidereal condition, and its final liberation through initiation. Reaching the upper extremity of the intellectual sphere, the candidate is incapable of further function, and swoons.

Upon regaining consciousness he discovers himself to be invested with a starry garment, the same spoken of by Apuleius in his *Metamorphosis,* and also that worn by the adepts of the Mithraic Rite. By the starry garment is represented not only the auric body but the new universal aspect of being—the sidereal consciousness bestowed by the experience of initiation. The candidate may return to the narrowness of his physical environment, but he can never again reduce his consciousness to the limitations of the material state. The starry body is his regenerated and illumined intellect.

The strange characters signifying the name of the *bird* with the green branch are decoded to mean "To be given the life"—that is, immortality. The name of the *altar* reads: "The Crown, Kether" and is decoded, "When shall be the gate of entrance." Together, the two phrases mean: "Immortality shall be conferred at the gate of the House of Wisdom." The name of the *torch* is *Light;* but translated, the characters read: "The dernier shall be hidden away and forgotten." This coin of the prophet should be understood in the sense of the suit of Coins in the Tarot deck, for this suit represents the material body over which the symbol has rulership. The statement may then read: "The body of the wise man shall be concealed." This thought was faithfully followed by the old adepts. The tombs of the Initiates have never been discovered; and in the famous Rosicrucian cemetery the resting places of the Brothers are marked only by the Rose. During the initiation ceremonies, which took place in the invisible worlds, the physical body of the neophyte was hidden in a secret place where no disturbing forces could reach it while the soul was exploring the mysteries of Amenti. Body here also represents personality and the whole personal sphere of life which must be cast aside and forgotten; also the personal ego which must die or be buried that the Universal Self may be born from its seed.

SECTION VI.

(*Figure VI,* page 43)   The altar which our author describes as being composed of the four elements is triangular in shape. From this circumstance two sacred numbers are produced: the square 4, plus the triangle 3, equals 7; and the four elements of the altar multiplied by the triangle equals 12. From this the composition of the world is made apparent. Nature is a triangular arrangement of four elements; and the divine world, of which the zodiac is a proper symbol, consists of these elements multiplied three times, or in their three primary states. The altar is the human body; its material parts—the square—are arranged in the spiritual order—a triangle. Upon the altar are the three symbols from the previous diagram. They are so placed as to form a triangle, and we must understand them as salt, sulphur and mercury—body, spirit and soul.

In the air above the altar is the crux ansata, the symbol of generation and fecundity. This may be considered as copper —the metal of Venus, and a symbol of the reproductive energy of the soul. Venus is the Lucifer of the ancients, the light bearer, the star of self-knowledge. This symbol must remind the sage that the power to multiply is common to both the internal and external man. As bodies generate bodies, so the inner body, the soul, generates the archetypes of personalities.

By alchemy, wisdom perpetuates itself by applying to its own peculiar purposes the same laws by which forms are perpetuated in the corporeal sphere.

The whole figure is a symbol of spiritual generation, the mystery of Melchisedek, who is his own father and his own mother and is above the law. It sets forth perpetual reenergization by the use of the Stone. It tells of the very power, which St.-Germain himself possessed, of continuing from century to century by means of the subtle Elixir, the secret of which was known only to himself and his Masters. First, the three parts of the composite man—spirit, soul, and body—must be brought into equilibrium, and from this equilibrium is born the Homunculi or Crystal Man. This Man is an immortally generating ego capable of precipitating personalities at will, yet itself unchanged by these personalities and unlimited by them. Instead of the soul living in the body and prisoned by its limitations, a new condition is established: the body lives in the soul. To the adept, the physical form is but an instrument for the expression of consciousness, intelligence, and action—represented by the *candle,* the *bird,* and the burning *altar.*

Analysis of the Text.

This part contains some of the most beautiful symbolism in the entire manuscript. The candidate, having transcended the four elements, now continues into the sphere of higher causations, where he is instructed in the great Cabbalistic principles by which the universal integrity is preserved. The *palace* is the archetypal sphere—Plato's world of Ideas. The simple geometric arrangement reveals the divine harmony.

The doors of the archetypal world swing open and the Hierophant of the Order comes forth. It is He who was called the Master of the Hidden House, the Initiator, the Keeper of the Keys of Thoth. Alchemy is a religion of fire, as is also Zarathustrism. The Magus therefore wears the insignias of Zoroaster and speaks in the language of the Fire Prophet. The names which the Hierophant gives to the *bird,* the *torch* and the *altar* are the same as those given in the preceding section.

In company with the Initiator the candidate enters the immense temple, whose 360 columns leave no doubt as to its identity with the universe. The altar already described, being the threefold cause of the material sphere, is placed in the center of the great hall. The Hierophant next informs the disciple as to the new names which have been bestowed upon the sacred objects. The *bird* is called *Ampheercha,* which is interpreted to mean that a mother shall bear the likeness, or double. This is a reference to the Immaculate Conception and to the Secret Doctrine as the mother of the adepts. The name for the *altar* appears to be the word for *priest* but refers to the Initiator as the one through whom the disciple is born in the second or philosophic birth, a mystery more fully explained in the name of *torch.* The hall is called *Sky* (the firmament) but involves in the formation of its characters the Cabbalistic admonition: "Worship the glory which is to come." The triangular altar is Athanor, a self-feeding digesting furnace used by the alchemists, but the word may be divided into two. The first part then means immortality and the second, the four quarters of the heavens.

The eighty-one Thrones placed within the palace of the Sky, each at the top of nine steps, are of great significance. The Rosicrucian Mysteries consisted of nine lesser and three greater rites or degrees—a system which may be traced directly to the Cabbala. Out of Kether, the universal Crown, issue the nine Sephiroth and from each of these in turn issue nine others. Nine is the sacred number of Man, and in the old Cabbala, Adam (ADM) is the numerical equivalent of 1, 4, and 40—numbers whose sum is 9. The symbolism of the nine is continued throughout mystical literature. The Eleusinian Mysteries were given in nine nocturnal ceremonials to represent the months of the prenatal epoch. By Cabbalistic addition, eighty-one equals nine, and the Thrones signify the eighty-one branches growing upon the great World Tree. The schools of the Lesser Mysteries are patterned from the universal harmony and here we see set forth the arrangement of the secret Brotherhood.

The name for the great hall is repeated in the text as the point where the venerable members of the school enter and take their seats. The disciple receives his philosophical name. He is called the Wise Man and the words mean: "To be the Face or Manifestor of the Most High." The nine masters of the lodge then bestow their gifts. The first gives a cube of gray earth representing the element of earth; the second, three cylinders of black stone—the three phases of the Moon; the third, a rounded crystal—Mercury; the fourth a crest of blue plumes—Venus; the fifth, a silver vase—the Sun; the sixth, a cluster of grapes—Mars; the seventh, a *bird*—Jupiter; the eighth, a small *altar*—Saturn; and the ninth, a *torch*—the fixed stars. For the understanding of the significance of these gifts, consider the following fragments from the Pymander of Hermes relative to the ascension of the soul through the nine spheres and its return to the Lords of each of these spheres the gifts or limitations which are imposed by the laws of generation:

"After the lower nature has returned to the brutishness (the elements) the higher struggles again to regain its spiritual estate. It ascends the seven Rings upon which sit the Seven

Governors and returns to each their lower powers in this manner: Upon the first ring sits the Moon, and to it is returned the ability to increase and diminish. Upon the second ring sits Mercury, and to it are returned machinations, deceit, and craftiness. Upon the third ring sits Venus, and to it are returned the lusts and passions. Upon the fourth ring sits the Sun, and to this Lord are returned ambitions. Upon the fifth ring sits Mars, and to it are returned rashness and profane boldness. Upon the sixth ring sits Jupiter, and to it are returned the sense of accumulation and riches. And upon the seventh ring sits Saturn, at the Gate of Chaos, and to it are returned falsehood and evil plotting.

"Then, being naked of all the accumulations of the seven Rings, the soul comes to the Eighth Sphere, namely, the ring of the fixed stars. Here, freed of all illusion, it dwells in the Light and sings praises to the Father in a voice which only the pure of spirit may understand."

The name for the cube of gray earth relates to the mystery of the spiritual birth; that of the three black cylinders is selflessness; that of the rounded crystal signifies the end of the ages or the cycles; that of the blue plumes is Aquarius or the Leg of the Great Man; that of the silver vase is the birth of the spirit; that of the grapes is regeneration; that of the bird, they who live in the light or truth; that of the altar, the fruitage of virtue, or ultimate good; and that of the torch "the springing forth," the Egyptian *Coming Forth by Day*—the completion, the ninth mystery. That the torch is really a symbol of the sphere of the fixed stars and of the corresponding strata of the human soul is further proved by the fact that the manuscript tells us that it is composed of brilliant particles.

The mystery of the nine parts of the soul constitutes the completion of the Lesser Mysteries and the full control of all bodily faculties, functions, and powers. The three Greater Mysteries lie beyond and are still symbolized by the *bird,* the *torch,* and the *light.* The Lesser Mysteries are rituals of self control and purification; the Greater Mysteries are rituals of creation. In nine processes man purifies himself, but only to the few are given the keys of the threefold creative Mystery: the creation of form, the creation of thought, and the creation of consciousness. Before leaving the chamber of initiation, the candidate drinks of the Water of Life, the nectar of the gods, which is explained by the philosophers as representing the blood of the Logos or the Sun—the divine energy which sustains the elect, and which is constantly flowing in the Grail of the Mysteries. According to the Greeks, the gods partake of no mortal food, but are nourished from the fountains of Eternal Good which spring up in the midst of the worlds. Having given the secret sign to the adepts, the new Initiate departs from the chamber by the right-hand path.

SECTION VII.

(*Figure VII,* page 54) The key to the seventh plate is equilibrium, this being the virtue bestowed by the seventh sign of the zodiac, Libra, the Balance. Our author tells us that the central motif, two small circles and a pendant cross, is a sacred seal. This may be interpreted as the celestial sulphur and salt —the Sun and Moon. The suspended cross is the Lapis Philosophorum, of the regenerated elements—*salt* (earth), *sulphur* (fire), *Mercury* (air), and *Azoth* the æther (water of the sages). The Sun and Moon are the father and mother of the Philosopher's Stone. They represent heaven and earth, from which is generated the cross—man, the progeny of the two immortal agents, spirit and matter. The cross also signifies the equilibrium of man suspended between his origin and destiny. The arrangement of the figures indicates the adept in whom the union of all opposites has been effected. The Initiate is the rational androgyne.

Surrounding the central part of the symbol are two circles of figures. The inner circle is composed of cuneiform characters; the outer, of hieroglyphics derived from several ancient languages, arranged in a manner entirely arbitrary, and undecipherable without the original key. The circle of cuneiform characters must be interpreted by discovering the Hebrew equivalents of the arrow-pointed letters. The text is apparently prophetic, and at first reading may seem to refer to the cosmic change which arises from the tipping of the celestial Balance. In reality, however, the material deals strictly with changes which are to take place in the soul of the Initiate. The cuneiformed-Hebrew reads as follows, probably continuing from the outer circle of hieroglyphic text:

"And is the outbreathing of Everlastingness. Know that place (sign or symbol, probably a zodiacal constellation) to be the end (of the ages). The Leg (Aquarius, probably referring to the Aquarian Age or cycle) is the beginning of the destruction." In the zodiacal ᴗycle of adeptship, Aquarius is the symbol of the final disintegration of the personality, for beyond it lies only Pisces, the Nirvana.

St.-Germain's manuscript also describes an axe, not shown in the illustration. This is the instrument of separation, and would agree exactly with the interpretation of the figure. This whole device is suspended between two pillars of green marble. These may well be the Jachin and Boaz of Freemasonry. Students of the Cabbala will remember the third column which united these two, and which, like the great seal in this figure, represented the adept whose perfected constitution united wisdom and generation—the law and the prophets.

Analysis of the Text.

The Initiate again assumes the attributes of the alchemical substance from which the Universal Stone is to be prepared. The entire section is devoted to processes of purification, consisting of three baths. As the result of the first bath, the water in the steel vessel becomes discolored with the impurities given off by the philosophical *matter*. In the second bath the elements of the Stone are impregnated with a mysterious reddish liquid of an extremely corrosive quality. In the third bath the corrosive principle is washed away. These three processes, which require sixteen days, completely purify the *matter*, which then passes on to its next augmentation.

From a mystical viewpoint, the vessel filled with crystal-clear water is the laver of purification placed in the courtyard of the Tabernacle of the ancient Jews. The high priests who served the Lord must cleanse themselves with the water from the laver before they could perform the sacred duties of their office. The ceremony of baptism is but the outer symbol of the inner truth. The Absolute Cause of all things in its impersonal and utterly diffused condition was regarded as a vast ocean filling all space. The Schamayim, which is the divine fiery water—the out-flowing of the Word of God—descends from the divine Presence. Dividing in the middle distance between spirit and matter, it becomes solar fire and lunar water. This Schamayim was known to the alchemists as the Universal Mercury, and is called Azoth, the measureless Spirit of Life. This spiritual fiery, original water passes through Eden (which in Hebrew means "vapor") and pours itself into four main rivers—the elements are the conditions of the Universal Mercury. This is the *tincturing water* by which the righteous are baptised. It is this water, the Universal Mercury, the solvent of the sages, by which the spiritual baptism is given.

He who is immersed in this water, or who receives the heavenly Schamayim into himself, becomes cleansed and purified. This Schamayim contains within itself the twofold baptism. Its lunar power baptises with water—the baptism given by John the Baptist; but its solar principle baptises with fire—the Messianic baptism.

The Initiates of the ancient Mysteries being lifted up into an apotheistic condition, received the divine baptism. They were immersed in God, and by this immersion they were washed clean of the black spot of original sin, which, according to Mohammed, is in the heart of every mortal. The Schamayim of the alchemists is the Shining Sea of the Buddhists, the boundless Nirvanic ocean, the water of space constantly alight with God.

The silver axe with blue handle, attached to the column, is called *the destroyer;* but the translation is: "Lift the voice to its fullness in chant. (Or song)." The axe is the ancient symbol of the Initiated Builders, the "hewers of wood." It is also the emblem of separation or division, and is an appropriate figure to represent separation through purification.

The sign of Libra, which rules the seventh operation of the philosophical mystery, divides the lower from the upper hemisphere of the zodiac. It is also the ancient sign of the Passover, a feast which signified the passing over of life from a material to an immaterial condition by the alchemical baptism. The gross particles of the soul are washed away and life is prepared for a supersubstantial existence.

SECTION VIII.

(*Figure VIII,* page 60)   In the sky blazes the philosophical sun, within it the face of the Logos. Its rays are concealed by the same clouds which must ever hide the Divine Light from the eyes of the profane.   The Lion is now crowned, its coronet having seven rays, symbolic of the seven energies of the will. This is no longer the despotic lion of the earlier illustration. Ambition has been transmuted into aspiration; and that impulse which, unregenerated, lures men on to temporal destruction, is now the force which bestows courage upon spiritual enterprise.

The bunch of grapes symbolizes illumination.   A curious work on alchemy states that the grape has a special affinity for gold, and that when vineyards are planted in areas where gold is abundant, the roots of the vine absorb the minute particles of this precious metal and distribute them throughout its stalk, leaves, and fruit.   In alchemy, gold is the symbol of the Supreme Principle.   The Nazarene likened His disciples and Himself to a vine with its fruits.   The grape cluster is an appropriate symbol for the school of the adepts, for the Initiates grow together upon a single branch.   Here also is a subtle allusion to the blood, which carries within it the golden particles of the sun.   The lion and the grapes restate the old formula—wisdom and generation.

The panels of characters on either side of the brazier contain fragments from old rituals and mystery texts.   The one upon the right reads: "Kindle a light at the appointed time— the seventh hour of the dawning."   This is followed by an obscure reference to the coming forth of fire at the full sun (noon) and the panel concludes with the admonition: "Dance in a circle and prophesy."

The panel at the left is also descriptive of a ceremony: "Honor is paid to the Giver of life."   The Initiate is admonished to sacrifice his Ka or soul.   The number 9 appears, and the symbol of the ark or coffin in which candidates are buried in the mystery.   Then the full face of the sun appears, to represent resurrection. There is an allusion to the gate in the heavens and the ascension of the Ka. With the aid of Egyptian metaphysics, it is not difficult to decipher these symbols. The number 9 refers to the nine Lesser Mysteries associated with the box or coffin—the body. The sun-face is the resurrection, and the whole panel describes the passage of the soul (Ka) through the invisible worlds as set forth in the symbolism of the Pyramid Rites. This is appropriately placed in the eighth division of the manuscript, inasmuch as the eighth sign of the zodiac is Scorpio and it was in a certain degree of this sign that the high priest released the Ka of his disciple into the Amenti.

Analysis of the Text.

The eighth section of the manuscript is devoted largely to an understanding of the mystery of the alchemical *salt*. Of this mystery of alchemy Eliphas Levi writes: "To separate the subtile from the gross * * * is to liberate the soul from the prejudices and (from) all vice, which is accomplished by the use of Philosophical Salt, that is to say, Wisdom; of Mercury, that is, personal skill and application; finally, of Sulphur, representing vital energy and fire of will. By these are we enabled to change into spiritual gold things which are of all least precious, even the refuse of the earth." The Salt of the sages is wisdom derived from experience, for experience is the salt of earthiness, or the material state, and a wise man is the salt of the earth. In our manuscript the salt is called "the first among the regenerated." When the Initiate impregnates himself with salt, it is equivalent to saying that he makes wisdom part of himself. Salt is a preservative of bodies, just as wisdom is a preservative of souls. Decay cannot affect that one who has discovered the *wise man's salt.*

Leaving the circular apartment and the mass of white and

shining salt, the Initiate approaches the edge of a somber lake, and perceives at a distance a bridge called *the strong to be subdued*. The term also signifies a reflector or a shadow suspended over the lake, and betokens the Rainbow Bridge, the Bifrost of the Scandinavians—the bridge which leads from earth upward to Asgard, the terrestrial paradise where dwell the twelve Ases, the Hierophants of the world.

The eighth sign of the zodiac is Scorpio, well represented by the dark and somber waters. The sign of Scorpio was especially venerated by the Rosicrucians, who performed certain of their rituals only when the sun was in this constellation. With great difficulty the Initiate forces his way through the morass of Scorpio to reach the great temple of Sagittarius which looms in front and above.

SECTION IX.

(*Figure IX*, page 65)   As this section signifies Sagittarius it is most appropriate that the figure of a horse should appear in the symbolism. The Trojan Horse, concealing within its body the army of conquering Greeks, represents the occult force of this constellation by which the Trojans (the material world) fighting to defend Helen (the lunar principle) were finally overcome. In astrology the ninth house, which corresponds to Sagittarius, is the house of the sacerdotal class, the priesthood, or the Mysteries. The hollow horse with the men inside is, therefore, the temple and its adepts.

In our figure, an unusual application is made of this symbolism. A corpse is falling from the horse. Beyond the ninth degree the physical body cannot go, therefore it must here be cast off. Form can go no further—the corpse is cast out of the temple.

The Arabic text at the top of the plate reads: "That which

is hidden shall be brought to view" or "the hidden things (sins) are to be stripped off." The cuneiform consists of the following legend: "The gate of the end (completion or conclusion) when the Leg or the Waterman turns in the circle (the equinox in Aquarius)." In the boxlike frame is the following: "The select few—how many are there? Forty who in brotherly love assemble together to the four quarters and the Bird. Here below (in the mortal sphere) to be held (gathering or assembly) until in its place is the coming in the fourth quarter (Aquarius)." The large characters MB refer to the alchemical process whereby the mortification and destruction of the body is accomplished. The floriate letters are words to be completed by the addition of other letters. When this has been done, the sentence reads: "Seek after the all-powerful Lord who is the guardian of the Tree of Life." In the lower half of the figure a red-robed man is attempting to restore life to the corpse. This is *fire* (or iron) striving to revivify the *ashes,* an alchemical emblem.

Analysis of the Text.

In the ninth step of the ritual, the Initiate comes face to face with the last great enemy—death, which must be experienced, understood, and overcome. In the gloom of the great chamber with its ebon walls he perceives the strange Horse of Troy. Here is *putrefaction,* the end of all ignorance and the gate of life. The Initiate spends nine days in the contemplation of this mystery, and is about to take up some of the foul and disintegrating *substance* lying piled in a corner, when he is warned by an invisible voice that the time has not yet come.

In Sagittarius, the ninth sign of the zodiac, the theory of philosophy is perfected, for the world was created in six days but *Art* is perfected in nine. Hermes writes thus: "But this

multiplication (the augmentation of the Philosopher's Stone)
cannot be carried on *ad infinitum,* but it attains completeness
in the ninth rotation; for when this tincture has been rotated
nine times it cannot be exalted any further, because it will not
permit any further separation." After theory comes practice,
after operation follows use. The adept, realizing that he already possesses the power to tincture matter, would experiment
with the black decaying earth in the ninth chamber, but is pre-
vented from so doing. He must yet receive the three Greater
Keys, for the power to accomplish transmutation is imperfect
until spiritual vision reveals the proper ends which the adept
must accomplish.

After leaving the house of putrefaction the Initiate observes
that his robe changes color, becoming at last a beautiful green.
This is a direct allusion to the alchemical formula. We are
told that during the processes of digestion the alchemical substance changes color, which has given rise to its being called
the peacock because of its iridescence during one of the periods
of its digestion. The various colored garments worn by the
several degrees of the ancient priestcrafts represented stages of
spiritual unfoldment. According to the same rule, in the preparation of the Wise Man's Stone the base substance passes
through a philosophical spectrum, turning from one color to
another according to the end which the operator desires to
achieve.

The three cryptic words with which the section is conclud-
ed cause the last sentence to read: "The name of the hall is
corruption. The name of the first lake is the beginning of
corruption, and the name of the second lake the end of corruption." The three cypher words, when connected. give the
meaning: "Corruption is the beginning of decay and corruption is followed by death." In the perfecting of the Stone of

the Wise Man is was discovered that it is impossible to unite the various elements into new fundamental patterns until each has been reduced to its most simple and original condition. This reduction, or the destroying of the personality of the elements, is the philosophical *corruption* which, brought about by *Art,* destroys all the apparent differences in the alchemical materials, and renders possible a perfect mingling of their principles to eventuate in the formation of the divine Stone. Mystically, the philosophic death is the destruction of the numerous aspects of the personality, so that from the soul and its extensions (the divine elements) may be formed the Diamond Soul of the Rose Cross.

SECTION X.

(*Figure X,* page 73)   A man robed in a green garment edged with gold, and bearing a lance, is arising amidst vaporous clouds from an open sarcophagus. Above the human figure is suspended a golden crown of light. The whole symbolizes the annual rebirth of the sun in the tenth zodiacal sign—the winter solstice in Capricorn. As the tenth month of the philosophic year, this hieroglyph sets forth the first of the three Greater Mysteries which are presided over by the constellations of Capricorn, Aquarius, and Pisces.

The drawing depicts the final victory of the spiritualized soul over the limitations of the bodily tomb. The green garment reveals the adept to be clothed in his illumined soul, which is under the rulership of Venus. The breastplate bears upon it cryptic letters which mean LIFE. The Initiate has achieved immortality. For him the tomb will be forever empty. He has become one of that small band of the enlightened "whom death has forgotten."

The Arabic characters on the lid of the coffin admonish

the Elect that they should seize upon a certain undesignated mystery "when the sixth sign or age is to be the breath." These words evidently refer to the parts of a ritual. That which is to be seized upon is the "master secret of alchemy." The tomb is also the burial place of the master of magic whose dernier (or body) was hidden, according to an earlier figure. In one of the early Rosicrucian books is described a curious practice of the Brethren. They are said to have periodically retired into their *glass eggs,* where they rested for a certain number of years, after which they broke through the walls and emerged again. This allegory in turn alludes to the periodic withdrawal of the Mysteries from society and their reappearance after a certain time has passed." From the inscription we are led to infer that the periods during which the secret Brotherhood comes forth from its obscurity are regulated by the astronomical cycles of the zodiac. We may read from the symbols, "When the sixth sign is the life-giver I will come forth."

The hieroglyphics in the panel at the top of the page are descriptive of the philosophic resurrection. They read in substance: "To be freed with a shout of joy when the downpouring of the holy Spirit descends." There is also mention of a covenant of blood with the One at the time of the fourth quarter, that is, the Waterman with the Face. (Aquarius.)

Analysis of the Text.

Death is followed by resurrection. Man must die many times in order that he may finally achieve immortality. The butterfly which decorates the portals of the alabaster palace indicates clearly that the mystery of rebirth is the subject of the tenth initiation. "The three stages through which the butterfly passes in its unfoldment correspond to the three degrees of the Mystery School, which degrees are regarded as consummating the unfoldment of man by giving him emblematic wings by which he may soar to the skies. Unregenerated man, ignorant and helpless, is symbolized by the stage between ovum and larva; the disciple, seeking truth and dwelling in meditation, by the second stage from larva to pupa, at which time the insect enters its chrysalis (the tomb of the Mysteries); the third stage from pupa to imago (wherein the perfect butterfly comes forth) typifies the unfolded and enlightened soul of the Initiate rising from the tomb of his baser nature." (See my *Encyclopedic Outline of Symbolical Philosophy*.) The threefold mystery of the butterfly is further suggested by the triple colonnade separated by aisles and passageways.

The cryptic name of the hall indicates that it symbolizes the life cycle and also the sphere of retribution. Translated, it reads: "At the outpouring of the Almighty (the persecutors or the adversaries) shall be shut up and overcome." Von Welling, in his *Opus*, describes how the rebel angels—the elementary spirits—were locked in the dark elements of the material universe as punishment for their rebellion. Alchemy, then, is the art of purifying these malcontents and restoring them to their original celestial state.

SECTION XI.

(*Figure XI*, page 78) As the tenth illustration represents the final liberation of the Divine Man from his physical limitations, so the eleventh depicts the attempt of the intellect to break away from bondage to the animal soul. The powerful man with his girdle and helmet of iron, and his crest of red plumes, is the Demiurgus or Regent of the physical world, the governor of the senses and appetites. He is attempting to bind the spiritualized intellect to the rock of ignorance. The handsome youth bearing the caduceus is the philosophized intellect. The mastery of thought, which makes the mind a servant of the spiritual self, is the eleventh step of the old rite.

The whole phenomenal universe against which the neophyte has struggled through his eleven strange and arduous adventures is personified in the red-plumed man. Here the world is making its last effort to hold the escaping superman. The effort is vain. No chains forged of earth can restrain or bind the Philosophical Mercury. We are told that in the alchemical processes this subtle essence can seep through an iron vessel (the warrior)—or through glass or porcelain—and vanish, in spite of every effort to capture its quintessence.

The eleventh figure contains numerous extraordinary and impressive hieroglyphics. The characters on the shield include a crossed scythe and sceptre—signifying death and resurrection, or mortality and sovereignty. There is also the axeblade, the hieroglyph of the hewer, the builder, or the geometrician. The smaller hieroglyphics mean *egg* and *cave,* and the lunar crescent may symbolize either a lunar quarter or a gateway. These symbols unquestionably refer to steps in the initiatory drama.

The words in the panel at the top of the figure may be translated: "To be the sign of the Leg with Everlastingness, to pour out and to be the herald of destruction." The thought is evidently prophetic, referring to the destruction of the unrighteous in the sign of Aquarius, the constellation which rules the eleventh section of the work.

The writing below the figure is purely mystical: "It is given that the evil shall be trodden out in the sixth portico." The soul, in its spiritual cycle of regeneration, crosses from the lower to the upper hemisphere of the zodiac at the end of the sixth sign, Virgo, or the Virgin. This virgin is the mother of the Messiahs. As physical generation begins in

Aries, so the generation of the wise begins with the Mother (the Mysteries) from whom they are born into the celestial hemisphere. The old order cannot proceed beyond the sixth gate, for the seventh is that of the new man or the second birth—a mystery hinted at in our inscription.

Analysis of the Text.

The Initiate, departing from the palace of the resurrection, sees fluttering before him the mysterious bird *Ampheercha* which now, however, has the wings of the butterfly added to its own. The Cabbalistic meaning of the bird's name is: "A mother shall bear the likeness." The intellectual energy of the Hermetic Ibis is now perfected by soul power, represented by the diaphanous wings of the butterfly. Apuleius created the Psyche myth as a method of setting forth the Hermetic Marriage or the union of the reason with the perfected soul. This is the second Greater Mystery: the accomplishment of the philosophic androgyne, in which the male and female principles of wisdom—represented by the Ibis and the butterfly—are united in one creature.

The Initiate is told to seize and affix the symbolic bird. For nine days (degrees) the adept pursues the bird, which he finally forces to enter the tower named *corruption*. The symbolism then continues, clothed in alchemical terms. The tower is the vessel for further digestion, through which the elements of the Stone must pass before their final perfection. The Initiate drives a steel nail through the wings of the bird. The name of the nail is an admonishment to make haste and complete the operation. The bird is therefore crucified to the wheel, as was the dove of Semiramis, or Ixion. The name of the hammer means *to come forth and be manifest,* an allusion to the strength of will with which this final operation must be accomplished.

Alchemically, the substance represented by the bird begins to gleam in the retort. The luminous quality intimates that the soul power of the Stone is beginning to shine triumphantly and that the arduous operations of the alchemist are about to be rewarded.

The Initiate departs. Having completed the eleventh Mystery and fixed the power of the soul-bird so that it can no more depart from him, he passes out between two great pillars, and finds himself once more in the Hall of Wisdom.

SECTION XII.

(*Figure XII*, page 84)   The pilgrimage of the adept is at last completed. In the heavens blazes the philosophic sun—a triangle surrounded by a circle and a square, representing the union of the diversified elements of nature into one divinely radiant and effulgent power. The female figure is Isis—her body being no longer concealed by the black garment as in the second picture. She is Nature. With one hand she points upward towards the Divine Light which is her own Source, while with the other she carries three globes emblematic of the perfection of *Art,* the supreme Hermetic alchemy. The globes contain the three parts of the Philosopher's Stone, bound together by gold rings.

The "large strong man" is the Initiate himself. Through the meshes of his golden armor protrudes the blue undergarment, his starry cloak. In his hand he carries a white wand ornamented with magical characters. This is the insignia of of his rank, the baton of the adept.

The time for the twelfth and last step in the initiation is at hand. The crown which was previously in the heavens is now upon the Initiate's helmet. Isis springs into the air, lifting with her the new Master. Nature, the heartless destroyer of the ignorant, is the gracious servant of the wise. Led by Nature herself, and lifted by her from an earthly state, the Wise Man ascends into the presence of the three Masters of the Universal Lodge whose radiant sun blazes in the sky.

In the twelfth zodiacal sign, Pisces, the Nirvana is accomplished, the Stone is projected, the secrets of Nature are revealed, and the Initiate soars upwards with the triumphant declaration of the Masters: "Consummatum Est."

Analysis of the Text.

The Initiate now identifies himself again with the alchemical *matter* and enters a crystal retort resting in a sand furnace which keeps it constantly at a gentle heat. The name of the hall is "A place where drops trickle." The basin sustaining it is "the desert of blazing fire," or "the agent which enables the drops to escape." From the bottom of the glass retort, vapors are constantly ascending. The adept is lifted up, and after thirty-six days is borne to the upper part of the globe. The heat being reduced, he descends, and discovers that the color of his garment has changed from green to brilliant red. "The solution in the alchemical retort, if digested a certain length of time, will turn into a red elixir, which is called the Universal Medicine. It resembles a fiery water, and is luminous in the dark." (See *The True Way of Nature* by Hermes.)

The adept himself is now the Universal Medicine. He is the very substance which is for the healing of the nations. His crimson garment is the vestment of the Red Elixir. He has become the Ruby-Diamond. After gazing upon a hieroglyphical picture, by which his instruction is perfected and completed, the new master of the Great Work finds himself in the Hall of Thrones in the Wise Man's House.

He beholds the *bird,* the *altar* and the *torch* united into one spiritual body. Heaven, earth, and man have been united by the indissoluble bonds of Hermetic wisdom. The projection of the Stone is the final testing of the completeness of the Work. The adept strikes the golden sun, shattering it into fragments. In his role of the Ruby-Diamond the Initiate then touches each of the broken parts and they too become suns as glorious as the original. The sun here represents the germ of the Universal Gold or the divinity present in all natures. This is broken into fragments, in agreement with the Bacchic tradition that the solar energy was distributed throughout nature. The philosopher then touches the fragments, and each becomes perfect. The alchemist is master of his Art, and by virtue of the Stone he releases and perfects the fragments of divinity locked within each mortal constitution.

The Supreme Judge of all works decrees that the adept has completed regeneration and that the Work is perfect. The children of light—his brother Initiates—hasten to join him. The gates of Universal Life are open, the veil of the mystae is lifted. The adept is now an epoptes—one who sees clearly. The elemental spirits symbolizing bodily limitations acknowledge the mastery of the inner principles. The philosophic birth is complete. The ages acknowledge a new Master.

Manly P. Hall published a quarterly called the *PRS Journal* for fifty years until his passing in 1990; most of the articles were from his own pen. With such an intimate association it would have been difficult to continue the same model, so a new magazine was born, *Ancient Wisdom for Modern Living,* with articles from the archives of Manly Hall's writings, as well as by other selected authors. The magazine also contains news and information about the Society, and a complete schedule of lectures and events.

To receive a **free** copy of *Ancient Wisdom for Modern Living,* or to request a complete catalog of books and tapes available, call or write to the Society at the address below.

Mr. Hall devoted the last few years of his life to developing and establishing a Home-Study University program. This program, *Learning to Live by Living to Learn,* was designed to assist the individual seeker in his or her quest for a better life, using the resources of the ancient wisdom teachings for guidance. The importance of personal experience and knowledge is stressed. As Mr. Hall said: "There are within us undeveloped spiritual energies and potencies that can heal the body and preserve the soul. The purpose of this education program is to guide these energies into conscious intelligent action for the benefit of all humanity."

The Home-Study University was founded on the premise that education continues long past youth when life itself is seen as the path of learning. Expanding upon the old slogan quoted by Mr. Hall in his last letter—"Only those who live the life can know the doctrine"—the course features the application of the ancient mystery teachings to the individual life. In this way, the knowledge of the ancient teachings can have practical significance and will make a positive contribution to the intellectual and moral climate of the twenty-first century.

Interested individuals can call or write to the Education Department at the address below:

Philosophical Research Society
3910 Los Feliz Blvd.
Los Angeles, CA 90027
(800) 548-4062 or (213) 663-2167